THE ROAD LESSONS TRAVELED

THE
ROAD
LESSONS
TRAVELED

*A collection of short stories
and reflections to find your way*

DIRK BROWN

Ripples Media

Travel leaves you speechless,
then turns you into a storyteller.

– Ibn Battuta

Published by Ripples Media
www.ripples.media
Atlanta, GA

First printing 2025

Designed by Burtch Hunter
Text set in Crimson Pro

979-8-9989701-1-5 Hardcover
979-8-9989701-0-8 Paperback
979-8-9989701-2-2 e-Book
Library of Congress Control Number: 2025915212

DEDICATION

To the adventurers Xenophon, Pausanius, Brendan the Navigator, Marco Polo, Ibn Battuta, Washington Irving, Jules Verne, Jack London, D. H. Lawrence, Freya Stark, Jack Kerouac, Michael Palin, and Bill Bryson whose travel writings I treasure. You have inspired me to keep my own journals.

To those precious souls who I have encountered in my travels. Your small acts of kindness are woven into the intricate fabric of my life stories.

To my family and friends who have listened to my stories. While I apologize that you are hearing them again, you have my deepest thanks for inspiring me to share them in print.

And to you, reader, whoever has ventured from home, whether across the street or across the globe. May my stories inspire you to travel more deeply and find your own words that we might journey with you.

CONTENTS

FOREWORD

–

by Autumn Phillips

Travel writing is a unique genre. Unfamiliar place becomes an armature to write about everything – personal growth, philosophy, politics, the taste of a freshly harvested tomato. Travel is such a good canvas, because – if you're doing it right – every sense is alive. The traveler notices the smallest details, relishes the mundane, lets the mind wander.

Writing forces the traveler to live more deeply and see more closely in order to make places and experiences come alive for the reader. Traveling in this way, with pen in hand, becomes a lesson in how to be more present back home, to slow down time and drink in every second.

Dirk Brown fills his pages with portraits. He is a people person.

For him, travel is a social exercise, to look at people closely and listen to every word.
As he travels, the places fade into the background as the faces come into clear focus.

During a student exchange in France, Dirk wandered into his host family's kitchen – against social convention – to spend hours with the cooks.

France comes into focus as he shells the peas, side by side, on those afternoons.

I can imagine how good it felt for those people to be with Dirk, to have someone really listen to their stories and soak of their knowledge. I imagine they still think about him from time to time, about how good he made them feel, how seen.

This book is a collection of travel writing and revisited journals, but it is also a rite of passage story as a young man learns about life and the person he wants to be, one journey at a time.

This isn't a tale of male bravado and adventure. There's a sweetness in it. As an adult, looking back at himself, Dirk writes with a vulnerability about his mistakes and a tenderness for his earlier self.

Dirk sprinkles advice among the stories, like how to get the best deal on a plane ticket. But the lesson I learned was the value of the list as historical record. Dirk has a compulsion to make lists and to hang onto them later. For example, he writes a packing list for every trip and then annotates it after the trip with messages for his future self.

These lists are full of the smallest details that would be forgotten if they weren't written down and saved. Of the people Dirk meets on his journey, one couple stands out.

Dirk and his female friend are in Paris, wandering among walls of art. They wore wedding bands on this trip to keep people from asking questions or raising eyebrows when they shared a room. The rings bonded them and projected an image to the world. An older tourist couple sees Dirk and his "wife" and immediately sees themselves in the young couple. They dive in with stories and advice. The encounter adds a layer to the theatre of the rings and gives them a Casablanca "we'll always have Paris" nostalgia.

But it's a growing up moment for Dirk, to understand how people jump to conclusions and only see through the depth of their own perception.

The Dirk Brown shelling peas in the French family kitchen at the beginning of the book is a much different person than the Dirk Brown at the end of the book.

What emerges from these pages is a profound truth: the most transformative stories don't come from exotic destinations or dramatic adventures, but from the quality of attention we bring to encounters. Dirk's gift, and the lesson he offers readers, is showing us that there is always possibility for connection, wonder, and growth.

We simply have to remain open to the people and the places we meet along the way.

—

Autumn Phillips is Editor-at-Large of The Post and Courier *and the 2024 North American Travel Journalists Association Journalist of the Year. She teaches travel writing workshops focused on finding deeper meaning in our encounters with the world.*

THE
ROAD
LESSONS
TRAVELED

BORN FOR TRAVEL

I am not certain that all these stories are true, but it is how I remember them.

I turned eight in the summer of 1969. My father decided that jet travel was the way of the future and that every businessman would be flying. Men would rule the skies as well as the boardroom. So he decided that summer was time for me to take my first step into the sky.

Jet aircraft started flying in the late 1950s in the US but did not start traveling the smaller markets until later. Eastern Airlines dominated the southeast, connecting cities small and large across the region and the globe. I grew up in Martinsville, a small Virginia city just over the North Carolina border. My grandparents and all my close relatives lived in the big city of Charlotte. My parents were the only ones to leave. Their own version of taking to the sky.

The closest airport was in Greensboro, and my father decided that my first flight would be between there and Charlotte. Today, you can drive between these two airports in an hour and a half on a Sunday. Then, Eisenhower's interstate system had recently been completed with the construction of Interstate 85. I am confident that it would have taken less time to drive between those two locations, but he wanted me to fly.

So, that summer, my father bought my first airline ticket in my own name, "Mstr. D. Brown." (In those days, *Mstr.* was a title of respect for boys under thirteen.) Today, children are born flying before they can even remember, but not in those days. Children were seldom seen and never heard. I remember that Thursday morning in June, full of clouds, sun, and anticipation. I remember dressing in my Sunday clothes, likely khaki pants and a blue blazer. Possibly my clip-on tie.

It takes under an hour to drive to the airport on Route 220. In 1967, the airport had constructed a new terminal and undergone upgrades to the runway to accommodate the new jet airplanes. In those days you could park right next to the terminal. The last time I flew out of Greensboro, there were still parking meters in front of the new terminal. I am sure that has all changed.

I clutched my tiny suitcase, hard-sided, and handed it over at the ticket counter. I remember the ticket, a paper sleeve with a carbon paper ticket written by hand. Those days, anyone could walk to the gate. My mother, my father, and my sister accompanied me right onto the edge of the plane.

At the gate, I was handed over to a flight attendant (referred to as a stewardess back then). In my memory, my father walked me down the gangway and onto the plane. *Was there a gangway or a walk across the tarmac?* The flight attendant walking with both of us. I am not even sure my father had actually been on a commercial jet aircraft – though he did train for the Korean War.

I remember meeting the captain and coming into the cockpit, looking out those big windows in the front. I may have even gotten wings to put on my lapel. And eventually, I was taken to my seat and my father left the plane.

Soon it came time for the plane to leave, the boarding door closed and I was alone in that big seat. The plane taxied down the runway and took off for its twenty-four-minute flight between the airports, wheels up to wheels down. Upon landing, the plane emptied and I was escorted into the terminal. Both of my grandparents were standing at the end of the gangway and I was once again in the embrace of family. This baby bird had flown the nest.

That quick trip made a lasting impression on an eight-year-old in several ways. My fear of flying predate ever leaving for that airport. Arthur Hailey's book *Airport* came out in the summer of 1968. A near-disaster story about a jet in trouble with a potential crash landing. Commercial jet travel was only ten years old and I wondered if my flight was going to be the subject of a real-life sequel. Fortunately for me and everyone else, mine was uneventful.

More importantly, I learned the freedom of travel and the experiences that come with it. Those twenty-four minutes were the first time that I had ever been alone while moving from one place to the other. I had been on car trips with my family to visit relatives or the school bus with my friends, but never with a group of total strangers.

The feeling of freedom overcame my fear and I have never looked back. Traveling alone is what caused me to face these two things simultaneously, with a little help from others along the way.

The only thing I have left from that day is the Eastern airline ticket. No photographs or wings, even the suitcase long gone. Holding it in my hand, the logo is faded, white and navy blue wings, with the name across the ticket jacket. The ticket is handwritten, with my name stapled inside. A flight of $17 in those days before the low fares brought on by airline deregulation.

Whether consciously or unconsciously, I decided that day that I wanted to remember my travels, capturing my experiences and hoping to learn from them. I set about to write all of them down.

. . .

My father loved amusement parks as much as I did. We visited Six Flags over Georgia in 1970. His sight was always on the holy grail of parks, Disneyland. For two years he saved his vacation so that we could take a trip to California, seeing all of America along the way. And in the early summer of 1971, with a pop-up camper in tow, my family left for a six-week adventure across America. I turned ten later that summer in August.

We made a wide circle, spending most of our time west of the Mississippi River. Driving the old Route 66, then replaced by the interstate going west, up the Pacific coast for the major cities of California and returning east along the remains of the Oregon Trail. Teddy Roosevelt would have been proud. We visited all the national parks along the way: the Grand Canyon, Death Valley, Yosemite, Yellowstone, and the Grand Tetons.

There are only a few photos of that trip. My mother's new 70mm video camera malfunctioned in the opening scenes of the trip. I have a small number of 1.5-inch x 1.5-inch grainy snapshots I took with my grandmother's small, automatic handheld camera. A very small visual reminder of a momentous trip.

Even without photographs, two important artifacts of that odyssey remain. One is a scrapbook of every place we visited. My mother collected ticket stubs, printed napkins, menus, and stickers to remember the trip. We placed them in a glossy, photo album upon our return. Secondly, for myself, I turned to writing a travel journal, though I did not know it at the time. Every day I kept a small diary of the places we visited, food we ate, and thoughts only a nine-year-old can think. It is a treasure trove of my early life and the chance relationships I encountered.

Other trip diaries follow throughout my early years. A trip to Williamsburg with my grandparents. A trip to Tennessee, interrupted by the death of my grandfather. All recorded in my cursive handwriting.

These travel accounts started me on a life of personal writing. We moved outside of Washington, DC, when I was in eighth grade and I suddenly found myself alone again. During this time that I missed my elementary and middle school friends, I turned to keeping a journal. It was short-lived once my social life picked up, but it necessitated the need to get my thoughts out of my head and onto paper. A chance to look at them and rethink how they might shape my worldview.

I started consciously journaling in the mid-1990s. Before that, I have a collection of writings on scraps of paper, napkins, and receipts, anything that could hold ink and was large enough to hold a thought. Most of them remind me of a time or a place, but always the experience that accompanies the moment.

My journals now take up nearly twenty-five volumes and an entire bookshelf in my library. Over those years, I have traveled to six of the seven continents, with my travels all captured in those books. I had never gone back to read them since they were written, and had very little desire to do it. Until now.

Why now should I want to plow through volume after volume, trying to decipher my handwriting across the world? Part of this is selfish. I want to translate my journaling into real stories that can be shared with a wider audience. Whenever I return from a trip, whether for work or pleasure, my family and friends want to hear my stories.

It is said that you experience a trip three times. First, when you plan the trip, envisioning it in your mind and placing yourself there. Second, when you take the trip, fulfilling that dream through intricate planning, no matter how it turns out. And third, when you remember the trip, looking at pictures or sharing memories with fellow travelers and friends.

On my last trip to Australia, I told work colleagues that I was invited to a reception through a chance encounter in a hotel bar. While there, I was introduced to the Lord Mayor of Sydney. One of them exclaimed, "Of course you did."

These stories long to be told. They make me laugh and cry and ponder as I read, remember, and write them. And I hope you will experience the same.

Travel is an experience that is deeply personal, yet also widely relatable. The stories of my trip to Ireland may spur recollections of your own trip to the Emerald Isle. You may remember when you had your first pint in a crowded pub full of traditional fiddle music. In that sense, while these are technically my stories, we can reflect on our travel experiences together.

My other aspiration with this book is to draw larger lessons from our travel experiences. I often find that people are more open to new foods, new adventures, and seek out new life experiences when they are away from home. I know that I do things while traveling I would almost never do at home.

Why? We are in a brand new, unfamiliar place, where we do not know anyone. We depend on other people, the kindness and patience of others. In response, we are kinder and more patient with ourselves. We also take the time to contemplate the world around us and our place within it. We travel thousands of miles to marvelous places where other people's lives take place. Through these interactions, we return home with a new appreciation for viewing the place where we live.

T. S. Eliot in his poem "Little Gidding" summed it up this way:

We shall not cease from exploration
And the end of all our exploring
Will be to arrive where we started
And know the place for the first time.

We should be fundamentally changed when we travel. After all, what is the point of investing time and money in visiting far-off places if we do not gain new understandings and perspectives along the way? What happens in Vegas – or wherever we have trekked – should not stay there.

But that is what happens with stories of travel and its lessons after we return home. The clothes are washed and packed away. The pictures are cataloged and stored. We return once more to our daily lives and the stories fade into a memory. Only pulled out on special occasions, like fine china, and briefly admired. Soon to be buried by the grind of our next initiative.

I am certainly guilty of this. We complain about the traffic on our way to work, days after appreciating the privilege of public transit to explore a new destination. After we happily unplugged and ignored our e-mail inboxes, once more our smartphone immediately becomes an appendage affixed to our fingertips. While we once wandered through public markets and curiously tried new local cuisines, we joylessly fall back to the same grocery aisles and takeout orders.

Part of this is natural. Our daily routines are how we stay productive. It is only natural to relish these comforts of home once we return back from our travels. My goal, however, is to encourage us to take that "wandering" mindset into our day-to-day lives. As someone who loves to travel, I believe that acting like we are on vacation when we are in our normal daily routines might make us happier, and without sacrificing one bit of productivity.

I remind myself that the place I live is where others travel thousands of miles to encounter what I see every day.

This love of storytelling and the collection of all

my travels captured in my journals form the basis of this book. I want to share stories that will entertain as well as inspire you. Most of these experiences have happened when I was traveling alone, open to the wider world of human interaction, with those whose culture and upbringing may be far different than mine.

I begin with the retelling of a story as best I remember, much like I started this chapter. You will encounter my travel experiences. Like learning to cook with the housekeeper in a French country house. Or bargaining for pearls in a jewelry store in Hong Kong. Or getting lost and hitchhiking in Ireland. I trust these stories will dredge up your own travel memories you have locked away for safekeeping. Now is the time to dust them off with me. You may even be inspired to pull out your own pictures and journals.

I reflect on the stories and reveal the lessons that inspired me – how these experiences changed me at the time and still impact my life today. If the lessons are not incorporated into my routine, then I should lean into them and make them part of my daily practice. We are called to live intentionally to get the most out of our time. Explore with me as we live our routine lives. In addition, you may discern learnings from your own memories and adopt them into your own daily life. Rest assured that I will leave room in my stories for you to find yourself.

I am a huge fan of museums and their staff, having done this volunteer role for an antiquities museum in Atlanta for many years. My favorite tour was the Saturday afternoon general tours. Once I greeted the group, I offered a glimpse into my touring style.

"For the next hour, we are going to journey together through ten thousand years of human history using objects from the museum's collection. I will not focus on dates and facts, but I want to give you the opportunity to encounter the objects. Who made them and how? Who used them and why? What do we use today that serves the same purpose?

"You may view the object differently once I tell you these stories. Even bringing in your own experience to play. When you next use its modern equivalent, you will remember these stories and see new life in a routine task."

As in my gallery tours, I serve as your interpreter through this book. I give tips and insights on my own travel, likely places that you have also visited. I want you to traverse your memory and encounter your own thoughts and reflections. Your takeaways and lessons may be similar to, or markedly different from, mine. These learnings belong only to you. And together, we will see our daily encounters with new eyes

More than anything, I want these stories to inspire you to travel even more. To travel solo if you are brave enough. If traveling with others, try to carve out time by yourself. Always leave space in your travel for what may come your way. If you are lucky, upon returning home, you will find your new learnings packed among your souvenirs, toiletries, and dirty clothes.

LEADER OF THE PACK

Ever since I can remember, I have been fascinated with all things French. As a child, I made my mother teach me every French word she could remember from her high school classes. In middle school, I created a scrapbook that included handwritten sections copied from books, including the Guinness Book of World Records. Did you know that Catherine de Medici, the queen of France, had a waist size of thirteen inches? Glued in the book were also magazine articles and newspaper clippings, anything connected with France. There is even a 1973 article about building a train under the English Channel to be completed before 1980. This scrapbook contained the first things that really brought France to life for me.

In the eighth grade, I took my first French class. I remember my French teacher, though I cannot recollect her name. A petite woman who demanded we speak mostly French in her class. I remembered speaking French in parroted conversations called *dialogues*. Through them, I learned that Sylvie was not swimming with Phillippe in the neighbor's pool, but was at the movies. We practiced them so much that I can still recite both parts. We counted numbers, learned verb tenses, both regular and irregular, and the whole world opened up through language. Learning to speak another language was a way of seeing as someone else does.

I continued to study French through junior and early high school until we moved to rural Virginia in tenth grade. The school decided to cut all fourth-year language classes, largely based on budgets, but also because most colleges no longer required four years of language for acceptance. I was able to continue my studies independently with the high school French teacher after school.

My father was a largely self-taught man from the school of hard knocks, though he did attend night school to obtain his associate's degree at my mother's urging. He never fully understood my interest in France, but he related to my burgeoning love of travel. He felt a similar call for the open road and never met a stranger along the way. To that end, he set about finding a way for me to travel to France – and extending the spring break weeklong tour. As the owner of a grocery store, he joined the local Rotary Club. He knew that the Rotary Club sponsored exchanges all around the world, largely for just the cost of the airfare. His goal was to apply for the upcoming summer exchange between France and the Virginia Rotary clubs as a way for me to get there.

In order to participate, our family had to host students from France. While the exchange covered families across the entire state of Virginia, most exchange students would stay in the suburbs of Washington, DC. My parents planned a summer of learning and travel for two students, one of whom would stay with us. So, in the summer after my junior year, two students from French Rotary families arrived in South Boston, Virginia.

To set the picture, South Boston is a small town of about 8,000 residents, located along the southwestern border. It lies closer to the capital of North Carolina than Virginia. Its historic neighbor just north of town, Halifax, serves as the county seat of the largest county in the state. A rural landscape of tobacco fields separated by deep hardwood forests, a lazy shallow river passes through it on its way to the ocean. South Boston lies on the route between the mountains and the port of Norfolk.

The trains full of coal would rumble past our house in the night, carrying their cargos to load onto waiting ships. I often walked that train track as it led all the way down to the river. I looked each way wondering where the track started and ended, what the train passed along the way and where its cargo was inevitably bound. It was my own imaginary travel in this very small town.

Here, two students from France would arrive in the hot summer of 1978 and spend the month. The student who stayed with us was named Gonzague, from a family in Grenoble. The other student from Toulouse stayed with another local Rotary family.

Flying into Dulles Airport, my family and I made the five-hour drive from South Boston to Washington to pick up the students. My father and I also took advantage of timing to see the arrival of the Concorde, its graceful landing with its nose high in the air.

Preparing for his university exams, Gonzague and I spoke mostly English, though we did find some time to practice my French. My parents only spoke English and my mother, a strict grammarian, was happy to point out the finer points of English to both of us. My father was just satisfied teaching him the culture of southern Virginia at our grocery store. We spent time stocking shelves and cleaning floors. At home, we worked in the yard and tended my small garden, as well as attending movies and dances. Gonzague got the opportunity to live the life of a typical American household – or at least ours.

On weekends, we traveled the state and shared our short history. One of the trips was a visit to Williamsburg, on the eastern side of the state. There they could see an overview of America from its founding at Jamestown to its independence at Yorktown, emphasizing the contribution of the French. After a day of touring Colonial Williamsburg and the historic houses, Gonzague asked about the importance of the site, remarking that his house was older than any building there.

At that point, I realized that our lives were so different. I learned that Gonzague lived in a small chateau. I say small, but when asked how many rooms it had, he responded that his family had never counted them. He sent us a postcard on his return with a picture of the house. Try imagining a place full of castles, and even a handful of dragons.

The following summer after my senior year, I got my chance to find out. The exchange would go the other way and send Virginia students to France for the month of August. Most would be staying with families around Paris. I had continued to write Gonzague and asked to stay with his family. Along with all the other things that typically happen in the final semester of your senior year, your last prom, your last papers and finals, your graduation and acceptance into college, I was accepted for the exchange.

I applied for my first passport and spent much of the summer working on my packing list. I consulted guidebooks and family friends who had traveled before to France. I remember that Americans were still afraid that the French had not fully embraced toilet paper and that I should carry my own. My mother made sure I packed an entire roll for the trip. A hair dryer with a converter from 110 to 220 volts was a must. My hair hung below my collar, like so many men in the 1970s. For Gonzague, a large jar of peanut butter, which was something he could not find in France. He ate it on everything once he discovered it at our house.

All of this in addition to a small pocket camera and rolls of film to capture moments of the trip visually. I bought my first travel journal, a small red journal handwritten in my architectural print, that would hold the written highlights of the trip. All these items packed in a large brown hard-sided piece of American Tourister luggage, loaned from a relative. That suitcase contained everything I needed for my trip, with additional space for any-thing I bought along the way for the trip home.

The day came for the flight, the second flight of my life and traveling further than I had ever been before. We loaded my luggage and backpack and headed to Dulles to meet the rest of the exchange group. Two British Airways flights, one overnight to Heathrow and a second arriving in Paris before lunchtime the next day. On that hot, late July af-ternoon, storms rolled in as they often do that time of year. The flight was delayed, but eventually, we were in the air. I remember a British dinner of beef, mashed potatoes, peas, and carrots. A screen pulled down in each cabin and a vintage movie for entertainment.

The late arrival into Heathrow the following morning allowed just enough time to make the flight to Paris. On landing, we passed through pass-port control to baggage claim. We had made the flight, but our luggage still remained in London. British Airways assured us that the luggage would arrive on the next flight. The next flight arrived; our luggage did not. For most of the group, the delay was inconvenient as they were staying in the Paris area and could retrieve it later. I, on the other hand, still had far to travel.

After waiting almost two hours, one of the French organizers came to me and said that I needed to get to the station for my train southward, assuring they would get my luggage to me. He put two train tickets in my hand, one from Paris to Lyon and then a transfer from Lyon to Grenoble. The family would meet me there.

He took me outside of the airport to the taxi stand to place me first in line. He prepaid the driver and told him to drop me off at the Gare de Lyon train station. Though I had never been in a taxi before, I settled into the back seat with a good view out the window. If I was going to see any of Paris, this was my only chance as the taxi would have to cross most of the city to get to the station. As we drove along the Seine, I caught glimpses of the Eiffel Tower, the closest I would get to it on this trip.

The taxi dropped me at the main entrance to the vast Gare de Lyon. Maybe there was just one train. No, there were dozens of trains. With much asking for directions in my high school French, I found my train, a modern electric train scheduled to leave shortly. I settled into a comfortable seat and promptly fell asleep. Somewhere south of Paris, I felt a rough tap on my shoulder. I awoke to the conductor wanting to see my ticket. "You are in the wrong class. You are in first class with a second class ticket."

Trains have classes? I thought. This car looked more comfortable than the others. After much apologizing, he told me that I could stay – and then asked for 24 francs, about $6. I paid him, not realizing that it would be the first of many travel lessons for which I would pay over the course of my years.

The train pulled into the Lyon station before nine o'clock, allowing twenty minutes for my transfer. In less than four hours, I quickly gained knowledge and confidence in finding not only the correct train, but also the correct class. The smaller lines were easy to find, the diesel train for my final leg of my journey. After the short hour-long journey into Grenoble, I disembarked. My host family greeted me with a handwritten sign and a warm welcome.

After nearly two days of travel, I had arrived, having mastered three modes of transportation, although without my loaded suitcase. Like any good Boy Scout taught to be prepared, I had packed a change of clothes and a toothbrush in my backpack, with my red journal tucked inside. In it, I made the first entry describing my journey in detail. The entry for that day ends with a single line, scrunched at the bottom of the page: "Overall, I loved it."

Through this experience I had risen to the challenge and overcome my first international travel experience. I found myself in a place that I had always read about, dreamed about, and finally I was here. I was able to experience it with a French family, to live life as they live.

I once read a quote that we are not travelers, we simply live in a place for a short time. For me, the key in this quote is the word "live." When we stay in one place for several days, we learn the neighborhood, including the best walking route to the bus stop and the aisles at the grocery store. We even recognize the dishwasher that lingers outside the restaurant on his break or the cashier in the local coffee shop. We make a connection, even just a glance or a smile. We know our way and put down our phone maps. You cannot hurdle through a place and think that you know it.

The Pew Research Center found that more than forty percent of American workers do not take all of their paid time off. Even more surprising, workers with higher salary and education use even less of their time. Compare this to Europeans, who receive four weeks mandated by law.

We therefore have a huge need to travel. To be away from the office and break our routine. When we take our precious time off and head out, we want to make sure that we make the most of our time away. Online tour aggregators list hundreds of experiences in any given place. Name an interest and they can provide a guide and an opportunity for that to happen, never lacking in something to do.

Similar to our time, we overpack our luggage, wanting to ensure that we have something for every experience – way more than we will ever need or use. I have always been a proponent of packing light. I rarely pack more than a carry-on bag, even if I am traveling for a month in the winter. It is a skill that I have honed over decades of travel with just enough luggage.

On my first trip with both my parents to Europe, I planned a seventeen-day trip to cover the highlights of Italy. My mother had traveled with me internationally and I knew her efficient packing style. To start, she placed the things for the trip on the guest bedroom bed. She had chosen darker clothes to hide smudges, limited underwear that could be washed out in the hotel sink, made sure everything could be mixed, matched, and layered.

Once she finished, I told her to take a third of the clothes away. She balked, though eventually relenting, and never mentioned it to me again. That is, until we arrived in Venice at the end of the trip. Over breakfast, she confessed to me that she still had one clean blouse that she had not worn. Indeed, I was correct about removing the clothes.

Overplanning and overpacking versus spontaneity and packing lightly. These are choices we make every day. How often do we overcomplicate our lives with our burdens of saying *yes* to everything? I am just as guilty. The responsibilities of work, family, faith, community, education, just to name a few. Not about getting ahead but just staying afloat. All the pressures that life puts on us and expects us to do.

Just like my packing, maybe we need to take a third away. Think about the commitments that we can put aside or offload to someone else. Or maybe we need to say *yes* to time for ourselves? To find time to travel spontaneously in our own lives? Walking away from our phones for a trek around the block or time with an adventure book. I love a long lunch with a good friend when I need a change of view.

We need to make time to practice unloading and lightening our daily lives. Not overburdening ourselves, unable to move quickly when an opportunity comes our way. To remember that we can pick up anything we forgot.

After my arrival in Grenoble, my host family began making calls early the next morning. After four days and many phone calls to British Airways, my luggage was located, just as it was about to be put on a plane back to America. The airline could send it to the Lyon airport and hold it there until we retrieved it the following day.

What had I missed in my luggage over five days? With just the few items in my backpack, I realized how little I needed to make it through the day in France. I did not need to have clean underwear every single day. There are washing machines to wash my clothes. I could even live without my hair dryer.

My journal captures the events of those luggage-less days. The days were filled with adventures, exploring the small village around the summer house, eating long multi-course lunches with relatives, and even attending Mass that Sunday. The lack of luggage did nothing to hamper living my life.

My mother has a saying about packing, but I think it applies to the journey of life as well. "It's not like you are traveling to the moon. They have stores wherever you're going. If there's something that you forgot or that you do not have with you, you can buy or borrow it on the way."

Lessons in Packing

—

I save my packing lists for every trip on my laptop. I have packing lists that are so old that they still include travelers checks, airline tickets, and travel alarm clocks. Things that are never used today, as my phone and debit card handle these items now.

My packing list reflects my desire to travel lightly. Each list references the location, the length of the trip, and the time of year. The packing list itself is divided into three sections: clothing, toiletries, and stuff.

For clothes, I always pack so that I can layer clothing as the weather changes. I make sure that all the colors coordinate, easy to mix and match. I usually pack a range from casual to dressy, and always throw in a bathing suit.

I often do small laundry in hotels. Body wash makes great detergent that rinses out well. And it smells great too. Roll your clothes in extra towels and squeeze out the excess water. Items harder to dry can be sent to the hotel or a local laundry.

I have a pretty standard list of toiletries and that rarely varies from trip to trip. It does include additional medications based on the climate and level of sanitation in the area of travel.

Under the category of stuff, the top of the list

includes all the electronics and their associated charging cords. Phone, laptop, digital camera, and earphones. Over the years, I have tried to simplify to fewer cords, though I still carry quite a few. When traveling abroad, remember your electrical adaptors. There is no need for current converters anymore with modern electronics. The current converter is built into the plugs for phones and laptops.

I now carry an electronic reader for guidebooks and leisure reading. For the latest guidebooks, I have found that the local library has a great selection that can be easily downloaded. You do not even have to go into the library.

Take the wooden utensil from your flight and carry a corkscrew to make a charcuterie for a lunch on the go or a rainy evening when you do not want to go out. You can carry a corkscrew in your carryon luggage as long as it has no blade.

Upon my return, I review my list, making notes if there was something that would have been useful or something that I bought while I was there. They form their own time capsule.

All these annotated packing lists give me a leg up

when I start to plan for similar countries, climates, and trip lengths. On a recent trip to Egypt, I started with my India packing list from a decade ago. The list required minor updates, mainly electronics, and, voilà, I had my packing list. Think how much easier that is instead of starting fresh each time.

FAMILY RECIPE

The host family who met me at the train station in Grenoble was not Gonzague and his family. As most French people take the month of August for vacation, his family decided that I would stay with two different sets of cousins initially. Three very different host families in all, finishing my time with Gonzague at his home.

To my surprise, the makeup of the Rotary Club's international memberships is somewhat different than the US. The US Rotary Club membership consisted of small business owners, much like my father. The French Club members, while still business owners, serve as CEOs of large corporations. Gonzague's family owned a pharmaceutical company in Grenoble where his father ran the company.

Gonzague's name was Derely and his family traced their name back to the late Middle Ages. I learned the "de" in his name denotes French nobility. The "de" became associated with nobility when two noble brothers shared the same surname. They would differentiate themselves by adding the name of the land they owned, or obtained through marriage, purchase or inheritance. The preposition "de" in French translates as "of" or "from." His last name, Derely, signifies his family was from the region of Rely.

As a note, the nobility as a legal class was abolished in 1790 with the French Revolution. Many descendants of these nobles are alive today and continue to associate with one another. I learned that they were fully aware of who would sit on the French throne if the monarchy were re-established.

Gonzague considered his family in the middle of the historical pack of nobility. His family made its fortune in the sixteenth century and their chateau, named Le Bachais, was dated from that time. As I mentioned earlier, when I asked Gonzague how many rooms his home contained, he replied that they had never counted – as if I had asked him how many pots and pans were in the kitchen cabinet. There was an entire floor that the family never visited. Gonzague and I worked with the gardener to prepare the grounds around the chateau for his sister's debutante party, held three days after I returned for school. They wanted me to change my plane ticket and stay. I sometimes wonder how my life would have changed if I had stayed. Today, the great park we gardened now serves as a public green space for the residents of Grenoble.

Gonzague told me that the middle host family was the most ancient family with the oldest name, also containing the preposition "de." It traced back to the fourteenth century with a chateau of equal date to match, known as La Commanderie. As I marveled at the famous painting of St. Gregory by Peter Paul Rubens on a visit to the Grenoble Museum, my host leaned over and asked if I had noticed the Rubens in their grand salon. In the chateau's library cabinets, I found documents that Cardinal Richelieu signed and sent to the family. There were stables with horses, as peacocks roamed the gardens. My bedroom furniture was made when the Europeans were settling the land that would become my home of Virginia.

The chateau today is now a hotel. My host's three sons now manage the property as their family has done for hundreds of years. Its grand rooms where we laughed and played cards now serve as the guest public rooms. Part of the lawn where they taught me the game of French bowling has been replaced with a swimming pool. My bedroom is likely still a bedroom. It would be something to see my companions and the chateau again in its new incarnation.

My first hosts, the Douillets, who picked me up at the train station that first night, had no "de" in their name. What they lacked in surname prepositions, though, they made up for in wealth. This branch of the family had made their money providing leather goods during Napoleon's campaigns. In the peace that followed, they became famous for their leather work. And when skiing became a popular sport in the French Alps, they shifted to making ski apparel. This business afforded them a very comfortable life.

I am confident that Gonzague wanted my initial stay to be with the Douillet family for two important reasons. Mr. Douillet had lived in Canada before settling back in France to run his company. He understood the North American mindset well and could translate my American-ness to his family. I remember him explaining my need to shower and wear a new set of clothes everyday (once I had my luggage). My overzealousness for cleanliness was only the beginning of our cultural differences.

Secondly, he spoke English as well as I did. When they picked me up at the train station that first night in France, it was his fluency in English that comforted me most. With his warm greeting, I already felt at home with this family. We drove an hour to their country home. Since it was nearing midnight and I'd had little sleep, they fed me a light supper and put me to bed.

. . .

The next morning I woke to my first French breakfast of eggs, croissant, butter, and home-made preserves. And my first chance to explore the house and gardens. The house, named Les Combes, had been in the family almost since the original seventeenth-century house was expanded in the mid-nineteenth century. A substantial house with sixteen bedrooms faced the main street in the typical manner of French houses. A stuccoed facade and a red terracotta tile roof. A large living room with comfortable furniture and a television, and a dining room with a French farm table that seated fourteen guests. A huge kitchen opened out into a garden lush with herbs and vegetables, flowers, and fruit trees. The sole purpose to feed the family and to beautify the house.

Mrs. Douillet and the three children were staying at Les Combes during summer recess. Mr. Douillet went into his office some days and always spent the weekends with us. I met the three children, Bruno, Ségo, and Éric. Bruno, the oldest son, was just a year younger than I was. While he had studied English for seven years, he and his father eased me into speaking French for the first time outside the classroom.

Another person also lived in the house with us. She was the full-time housekeeper and cook. She lived on property in the historic servant's quarters. When I encountered her, she was cleaning the house, cooking in the kitchen, or picking produce in the gardens. She never spoke and never looked at me, always stepping out of my way. A part-time gardener also tended the manicured lawn and garden. He never came in the main house, only the kitchen, and never spoke, just like the housekeeper.

During my stay, Bruno and his siblings were my constant companions. We spent our leisure time playing tennis at the house or windsurfing in the nearby lake. Learning the French version of Monopoly when it rained. The house was full of relatives, cousins, aunts, and uncles always staying for a meal. Most of our afternoons were spent at multicourse lunches in the garden. Mrs. Douillet put her sixteen bedrooms to good use for a long period of rest and quiet after eating.

For me, I struggled with this afternoon ritual. I have never been one to nap during daylight hours. My most productive hours of the day have always been the afternoon and evening. I wake up slowly and struggle most in the mornings. On a rare occasion, a power nap of no more than five minutes prepares me for the rest of the day.

My body clock followed its normal pattern there, even with the time change. While the family settled in for their nap, I would typically go to my room and read. When that no longer satisfied me, I would venture out into the house and gardens. Since the housekeeper and gardener were always busy during this time, I asked Mr. Douillet if I could help either of them with their work. He told me that both of these domains belonged to his wife and he needed to talk with her. He brought me with him while he talked with her. Mrs. Douillet quietly objected.

I stepped into a part of French culture I knew nothing about. The American South had its unwritten rules of place, but that all started to unravel during my short lifetime of the 1960s and 1970s. In France, I made the assumption that the same changes were occurring. It appeared that a society where the class system had supposedly been abolished since the Revolution was alive and well. Everyone in the system quietly played their part, staying in their own lane. I unknowingly broke those rules with my request. I just wanted to figure out how to spend my afternoons and I thought I might learn something in the process.

The conversation was not over, though I was excused from the room. I learned later that Mr. Douillet continued and his wife relented. I learned that he explained to her that Americans will talk to anyone, often not following norms of class and society. No matter what he said, I was happy that I could work in the garden and the kitchen, both places where I was comfortable.

Now for the next step in the process. Mrs. Douillet needed to explain to the gardener and the housekeeper that her house guest would be talking to them, asking them how to help them with their work. The gardener was used to working with others. I started in the garden, comfortable there, having a vegetable and flower garden of my own at home.

I spent my time weeding, edging, and picking vegetables that would be used for the household. The chimes of the church steeple clock noted the passing of the quarter hours. It reminded me that these bells had created the rhythm of the village for centuries. Mrs. Douillet found me old clothes for my garden work, letting me know she had embraced my choice. The kind of French the gardener taught was something I would never learn in school, only in experiencing real life.

The housekeeper, who had been more reticent to my involvement, grew to accept my comings and goings through the kitchen to my work in the garden and bringing vegetables into the house. She eventually relented and I became a fixture in the kitchen. It was natural that I should see how these vegetables were used in French cooking. Here was where I spent most of my afternoons. When I first entered the kitchen, the cook was very tentative, spoke very softly in French. I told her that I could do any prep work that she needed. Growing up as a Southern boy, I knew how to shell peas, snap beans, and chop potatoes.

Before long, we were working together, learning her recipes for the basic dishes of a summer meal. By the time I left, I was preparing her dishes myself that were served at the family table.

Only Mrs. Douillet entered the kitchen to speak to the housekeeper. I would hear them discussing food menus. The rest of the family sat at the large wooden table for breakfast; all other meals were served in the dining room. She respected the housekeeper and ensured the house was clean and her guests were well fed. There was still an obvious gulf between them, despite their conversations.

That large wooden table in the middle of the kitchen became my afternoon place. The cool ceramic tile running up the walls around me. The large stove with its gas burners and bubbling pots. The housekeeper would sing while she was standing over it, stirring to the beat of her song. Most of the time I simply observed her graceful movements and the tender way she handled the vegetables. She respected them, the land that had grown them, and the joy they would bring to the eater. It was my time alone in the quiet of the house. I needed few words,

French or English, while my hands were busy.

I learned how to make potato salad, cook those tiny green beans and dress a fresh salad with homemade vinaigrette. Many of these recipes I still make today. When I make them, they transport me back to that kitchen. My hands still know those motions that they learned sitting at that table. I often think I ought to sing while I am cooking French dishes. I still set my table with French porcelain and cutlery. Several years ago, I was given a vintage set of Julia Child's two-volume *Mastering the Art of French Cooking* for my continuing culinary education. After all, I, like Julia, was trained under a French cook.

I owe all these experiences and recipes to two women, one was Mrs. Douillet, the other one is nameless. I never documented the housekeeper's name in my travel journal. She is never mentioned nor is the time I spent in her kitchen. My journal is filled with Mrs. Douillet and her family, including all the events of my weeks in her home.

I am grateful to Mrs. Douillet for stepping out of her comfort zone to let me have time in the kitchen. Though at first she was reluctant, she overcame her own social norms so that I could learn from another woman – one who was supposed to be invisible to the guests. I am also grateful to the housekeeper for overcoming her hesitancy to interact with a guest. She shared her time and her recipes, ones that my hands still know by heart. Both of these women had a deep impact on my life and still do.

Purely by accident, I learned that I had broken the given cultural norms of their society. I had done what was almost unthinkable by asking a simple question. I sometimes wonder if I changed the dynamics of the relationship between those two women after I went home. Did they spend more time in the kitchen together, laughing and talking about village happenings? Did Mrs. Douillet introduce the housekeeper to her other guests?

As a traveler in this sometimes lonely world of ours, we never know whom we will encounter. Sometimes on days when I am trekking, I realize that I have hardly said more than a few sentences over the course of the day. Maybe we do this when we journey in our own lives at home.

We live in a world of unwritten rules. For many

of them, we may not understand them or simply internalize the reasoning for why they are in place. We just unconsciously abide by them. Until someone questions them, either overtly or, in my case, out of youthful naïveté.

There are certain rules, such as halting at traffic lights or standing single file in the post office, to which we all need to conform. If suddenly we all began to ignore those, chaos would ensue. Others, particularly those involving relationships, may not need to be so cut and dry. Society will still function if these rules are bent.

It is in this bending that we rise above our reticence and let our curiosity guide us. We may unknowingly meet someone or learn something that we will carry through our entire lives. Through that connection, we may change the way another looks at their own world.

Our country is deeply divided on so many levels – politically, racially, geographically, and economically to name only a few. We tend to stay in our own bubbles, in life and online. We cannot live that way and expect for our society to survive. Even the most introverted among us need human interaction. It is imperative that we see the other viewpoint and foster those relationships.

We encounter every day those whom we may view as different and often never give them a second thought. The wait staff in the restaurant or the maintenance person in our office. In this world where it is easy not to see, there are simple ways to engage. I try to make time to get into the human checkout line at the grocery, just so that I can talk to that person running the register. If only for the interaction to ask about their day. They often ask about mine in return.

There are also deeper ways to engage others we do not know. The most basic is service, particularly community involvement. When we serve together, we stand on the same side of the table, not the opposite. When we serve together, side by side, hands working in harmony, there is no room for divisions. We serve the common purpose of strengthening our community on many different levels.

Step out of your comfort zone and make that connection, even when it feels out of place. Give any excuse to experience what you have never seen or heard or tasted. It may change your life, and just like my time in France, it might turn out to be delicious.

Lessons in French Cooking

—

Mrs. Douillet's Housekeeper's French Potato Salad
Serves 6

Whisk together the following ingredients to make a vinaigrette and set aside:

- ¼ cup of olive oil
- 3 tablespoons of dry French white wine
- 2 tablespoons of white wine vinegar
- 2 teaspoons of Dijon or Old Style French mustard

Place 12-14 red potatoes (about a kilo) in a large pot of water and bring to a boil. Boil for 15-20 minutes until potatoes are soft enough to pierce all the way through with a fork. Remove from the water and drain. While still hot, cut the potatoes into large bitesize chucks (¾-inch cubes).

Toss the warm potatoes into the vinaigrette until the liquid is absorbed.

Mix the following into the potato mixture:

- 2 thinly-sliced scallions
- 1 teaspoon of fresh tarragon
- ¼ cup of fresh parsley

Season with freshly ground black pepper to taste (¼ to ½ teaspoon).

Serve immediately warm or at room temperature.

CHOOSERS CAN BE BEGGARS

The first time I heard a Greek myth, I must have been in the second or third grade. A librarian pointed me toward a copy of *D'Aulaires' Book of Greek Myths* in my elementary school library. Checking it out, I remember it as one of the largest hardbound books I had ever carried or attempted to read. The book was huge, like one of those oversized picture books several feet tall, spreading my arms wide to read it. Almost 200 pages! It would not fit under my arm or in my backpack.

Published in 1962, Ingri and Edgar d'Aulaires created the text and full color illustrations that were hand drawn. The stories begin with the myth of creation, the world out of chaos. The personified earth and the sky falling in love and creating all the other gods until finally Zeus triumphs over all. Action tales of the minotaur and the labyrinth and Odysseus sailing home from Troy. All of these drawings opened my mind to the world of the ancient Greeks. I have no idea how many times I checked it out that year.

Many years later in my twenties, I saw a reprint of the book in the Metropolitan Museum of Art catalog. I was volunteering as a docent at the Michael C. Carlos Museum for their fourth-grade programs and I knew I could inspire them with the book that inspired me. The day the book arrived, I tore into the package, a paperback edition. I stared at the glossy cover of Apollo as the sun god riding his chariot across the sky. I was transported back to an earlier age.

As I held the book, I was disappointed at the size of the book. Instead of the large book, it was slightly larger than an 8 1/2 x 11-inch sheet of paper. I could not believe they did not reprint it from the original.

I called my mother in excitement and disappointment. When I explained its size, she said "There is nothing wrong with the size. That was always the size. It is you who are different in size."

Again, it was a whole new perspective on an old friend.

Though I had changed, those illustrations and myths stayed with me. As I grew older, I devoured Edith Hamilton's *Mythology*, a must-read for anyone interested in Greek lore. I expanded my readings to include the stories of the Egyptians and Mesopotamians, the Mayan and the Indian subcontinent. I realized the Bible's book of Genesis as the early creation stories of my own present-day religion. These myths opened a glimpse into the lives of the ancients and their view of the world.

When I was fifteen, Egypt sent the treasures of King Tutankhamun for a US tour. I begged my parents to visit while the exhibition was in Washington, DC, at the National Gallery. On a cold January day, we arrived at 5:30 in the morning to take our place with those waiting to see the exhibition when the museum opened at 10. We entered the exhibit before lunchtime and marveled at the finely crafted pieces of an ancient life.

I thought of the words of the archaeologist Howard Carter when he opened King Tut's tomb and was asked if he could see anything. He responded simply with the famous words, "Yes, wonderful things."

I was swept up in the US Egyptomania of the mid-1970s. I repainted my bedroom and created hieroglyph stencils for the walls and furniture. I ordered bedspreads with hieroglyphs and scarabs, made to accompany the exhibit. I created large hangings of pharaohs to decorate the walls. In the spirit of archaeology, I went as far as venturing into abandoned houses to see what I could uncover.

As a freshman at the College of William and Mary in 1979, I decided to put away these childish interests and focus on what would provide a worthy career, mathematics and computer science. I did not take a classical studies class on ancient Greek art until my second year, but it was as an elective. Not as a main focus the way that computer science and math were – or so I thought.

With computer science, I took one coding class

during my freshman year. After using card punch machines and card readers in a time of Fortran, it was enough coding for my lifetime. I had no interest in signing up for the next semester.

On the other hand, I was drawn to mathematics. Its simplicity and perfection were elegant, describing the world around us in a language of numbers. I remained true to mathematics, declaring a major in the spring of my second year.

In the spring semester of my junior year, I remember sitting in an advanced multivariable calculus class taught by my math advisor. He asked a question about a triple integration of a vector in an nth dimensional space. When there was no answer, I raised my hand and quietly asked from the front row, "I'm not sure I understand the relevance of the question? There is no such thing as an nth dimensional space that I am aware of."

He responded, "Mr. Brown, please just answer my question."

I answered, "A straight line."

"Correct," he said, "and I will see you in my office after class."

When the bell rang, we walked to his office. He said to me, "You just are not getting into this math stuff at this point. You are so capable but you have lost the passion for it. What do you really want to do?"

I stuttered, "I want to be a classics major."

It was the first time I admitted this fact to myself, having even said it out loud. I told him I wanted to change my major after one Greek art class. He responded that he would help with the transition of all my work to start my new major. In the last conversation I had with him as advisor, he said that he admired me for following my passion, and that had he not been a math professor, his fallback plan would have been as an archaeologist.

Changing majors in the middle of my junior year, with only one class in that new subject, meant several things. First, I would have to stay an extra year in college to get in all the credits. Secondly, my last two years would consist entirely of classes in the classics department. I approached my Greek art professor and asked if he would serve as my advisor. While he agreed, I think he was as stunned as my math advisor. We planned out how we could do my entire major in two years. I worked the first year taking classes in Greek and Latin, ancient history, art, and literature. As the year progressed, I wanted to understand it more deeply and felt that I could only do it by being there. I began to research summer schools in Greece.

My advisor recommended me for a program sponsored through Harvard University. The school was located in the small fishing village of Galatas, a two-hour ferry ride across the Saronic Gulf from Athens. Inland was the ancient city of Troezen, where Theseus lost his sandal before his time fighting the Minotaur in Crete. A land of lemon groves ran down to the blue water of the Aegean Sea. In the midst of this scenery was the school, shaped almost like a pinwheel. The center formed an extensive library; the arms created outdoor classrooms separated by walls. Classes were taught in the open air in the cloudless sunlight of Greece. The professor list included a world-renowned scholar on ancient city planning and the local ruins provided the perfect classroom to study with him.

If the professor list did not clinch the deal, then the setting most definitely would. There was now the task of applying and paying for it. The application was one matter, but the funding was a different matter altogether. I was getting through college with a mixture of savings, financial aid, and employment, with no extra funds for a summer abroad. There was not only the cost of the tuition for the summer study, but also my flight to get there. Airline tickets were still expensive in the days before deregulation. My parents graciously offered to pay for my flight as my Christmas present. This ticket was a large step toward realizing my goal. It took a great sacrifice for them to come up with the money to support me in this educational venture.

There was one large hurdle left to overcome. I had to find the full tuition if I was going at all. All fall, I had asked everyone who had an interest in my education and generously offered a portion of the necessary funds. I applied for private scholarships. I had even attempted to save money out of my meager part-time jobs. Nonetheless, I still had nowhere near the amount of money that I needed for tuition.

My last attempt was the financial aid office for the university where I could beg for the rest of the money.

I made an appointment and dressed for success. As I sat down in front of the financial aid officer, I explained to her the opportunity to study abroad for the summer, even showing her the program brochure from Harvard. I had already tapped all of my financial aid for my school tuition at William and Mary.

She looked at me and said all the money had been disbursed for the year. The school was already into the second semester and most funding had already been distributed at the end of the first semester, with the remainder earmarked for the rest of the year.

I asked if there was anything else she thought I could do – any scholarships or alumni that could possibly fund my tuition?

Shaking her head, she indicated none of these options were possible. I was desperate. With all my best effort, I decided to try to cry. I imagined the saddest thing, which was easy since I would spend the summer at home if I did not get this tuition.

The tears began to form in the corners of my eyes. I could see a change come over her face.

She blurted that she would find the money, that she would find it somewhere. As she handed me a tissue, her eyes just pleaded with me to stop crying in her office. I continued to sniffle all the way out of the office and back into the hopeful world.

Within a week, she called to tell me that she had scraped together the bulk of the money. The rest would be my responsibility to raise. With saving all fall, I had enough to cover the rest of the tuition, plus a little extra. I wrote a check for the deposit. I felt I was already on my way.

That experience changed me, not just for the moment or the summer, but for the years to come. I learned something inside of me that I did not know that I had. To have the opportunity to learn, travel, and grow, I would do anything within reasonable means.

I was a scholarship student. I worked hard through my education to ensure I could get into a top-tier university. I chose William and Mary, a modern university with a tradition of classical education.

I was fortunate that public institutions of higher education in Virginia are some of the best in the country. The in-state tuition helped me pay most of my own way with the help of financial aid and scholarships. That covered the basics. All my life expenses came from countless individuals and family grants that generously helped me along the way to complete my degree.

The old adage says that it takes a village to raise a child. That was definitely true in my case and continues for me today. We are all part of that village, both as receivers and givers of support and encouragement.

What if we all worked every day to pay it forward for all the support we have received in our lives? It is so easy to get caught up in the hectic pace of our daily living that we do not always notice those little ways that we are supported. What if we took a day a week or just an hour, to notice the gifts, accept them graciously, and reflect them back to another? Simple things like remembering to say thank you or holding the door? Maybe that even means, though it sounds heretical, letting that car over that waited until the last minute to get into the merge lane. We could be so bold as to pay for the drink of the person behind us in the coffee shop line. It costs so little for us to be kind.

Think of someone who played a supporting role in your life, reach out and call, text, email, DM them. Do it today, not tomorrow. There is no time like the present. Tell them how much their support meant to you, how it changed your life. Letting them know their impact will change the rest of your day. I guarantee that it will change theirs too.

. . .

With the help of the scholarship, I traveled to Greece for summer study. The trip went beyond travel for leisure and casual learning. It set me up for the future. A future of travel that included formal study and eventually work. The experiences and the people I encountered in Greece will make appearances in forthcoming chapters.

Many years after graduation at a college alumni event, I ran into the same financial aid officer, the one that found the money for me to study in Greece. She had long ago moved into other roles at the college. We started reminiscing about my time in school and all my visits to her office.

"Do you remember the day that I came to your office because I wanted to study in Greece? And you helped me find the money I needed?" I asked.

"Oh, yes, how could I ever forget?" she responded. "To have a grown man breaking down in my office. It broke my heart to think that this was something that was so important to you. That you would sacrifice so much to study abroad. I wanted to make sure that you fulfilled that dream."

She paused and then continued. "By the way, I knew you were one of the good ones. One I wanted to succeed. I knew in your lifetime you would give that money back for education many times over. Especially for student travel. I think I made a great investment."

To her dismay, but maybe not her surprise, I felt tears well up in my eyes.

Lessons in Cost-Effective Travel Deals
—

On a recent trip, my spouse was telling our traveling companions that I had saved over $500 on each of our airline tickets. When asked how, he replied that I played airline and hotel rates like a day trader in the stock market. I cannot deny this is true.

Since the COVID pandemic, airlines have eliminated all the pesky change fees from changing a ticket. True, the airlines will often only give you an electronic credit in your wallet that you can spend later instead of a refund. If you are a constant traveler like me, you will use that credit in no time. Even if you are an infrequent traveler, you still have a year to apply the credit to another flight. Do not let this keep you from searching for a better deal.

You can book a flight up to a year in advance. I typically start looking about six months out for international travel. Black Friday sales are often a great time to book for the following year. Once upon a time, airline sales started every Tuesday and those were the best days to book. Today, there is no magic day or time to book. The day of the flight actually has more bearing on the cost. Flying midweek on Tuesday or Wednesday can save a lot of money, sometimes as much as fifty percent.

I will watch fares and use that to determine the right time to book. Some websites track prices to locations and will advise you to buy or not. Upon booking, that's when the day trading begins. Most airlines allow you to store the destination and the preferred dates for your trip. You can even set the search if your dates are flexible by a day or two. Every couple of days, I go into the website and check the prices on the flights.

I am amazed at the range of prices over a period of time. If the price drops, I will cancel the original flight and wait for the e-credit. Using the credit, I book the new flight, banking the new funds in my wallet for the next trip. On a recent trip to Egypt, the flight started at $1300. I eventually paid just over $800. That $500 credit paid for most of a flight to Ireland the following year.

For hotels, I follow a similar method. Since you only guarantee hotel rooms with a credit card, canceling and rebooking rooms is simple with no refunds. Checking the hotel rates on a regular ba-sis will result in big rewards, often saving as much as half the cost of the room.

In the end, my efforts at cost savings are about getting the most out of my travel budget. To have the money to travel more. Set your sights on your dream location and work as hard as you can to squeeze every dollar out of the cost to maximize your experience once you are there.

THE TALE OF TWO RINGS

Susan, a fellow classmate in my classical studies program at the College of William and Mary, was also studying in Greece the same summer, though at a different school. She was studying at the American School of Classical Studies in Athens, just a ferry ride from my school. I knew Susan academically from classes and field trips as well as having the same advisor. Outside of class, we served on several other university life committees, even attending weekend retreats together. Though I knew her, it is always an adventure to travel with someone for the first time. We tossed around the idea of traveling together to save money by splitting expenses.

Since our summer semesters started within a couple of days of each other in early June, we decided that we would travel together in May before our schools started. That gave us three weeks between the end of our American spring semester and the beginning of our Greek summer school.

Susan had never been to Europe and we decided to make the most of the cost of our flights. We planned our May time, flying into London and making our way overland to Athens. We would see the major Greek and Roman art collections along the way.

I had an opportunity to travel with my university choir for a month-long European trip the summer before. We traveled the capitals of the continent and the UK singing in both grand cathedrals and small parish churches. Always staying with a host family to keep the costs in check, the group had fundraised for two years to make the cost affordable. I was now the "expert" on European travel and set out to plan my first full trip with Susan.

London was an obvious first stop for its collection at the British Museum. Next stop would be Paris and the Louvre. Then a week in Italy, with its famous museums and sites, before arriving in Greece.

Susan grew up as the only daughter, having three brothers, in a conservative Southern Baptist family. Her family lived in the town of Lynchburg, Virginia, about an hour from South Boston. Think Liberty University and the Falwells of the 1980s. When she discussed the travel idea with them, they were keen to meet this young man that would be her traveling companion. Susan and I arranged a dinner during spring break where the two families could meet. A slightly awkward "I'm bringing a boy to meet my parents" kind of evening. I have had job interviews that were less stressful.

I must have passed the test as they gave us permission to travel together, even sharing that they felt more secure that Susan had such a fine young man to accompany her.

As a mental picture, Susan was a beautiful woman, slender, almost matching my six-foot height. A creamy complexion that never saw the sun. Full, curly blond hair. Never seen without a dress and often with a broad brimmed hat. She cut a striking figure in any room.

To seal the deal, Susan and I thought wearing wedding rings would reduce questions, particularly when sharing hotel rooms in the more conservative parts of Europe, namely Italy and Greece. I owned a single silver band that I wore on my right hand. It was easy to just switch it to the left. Susan purchased a fake solitaire ring for the occasion.

We met at Dulles and boarded our flight to London. A high school mentor and his family had been transferred to London for work and he offered to let us stay in their townhouse in London. We spent our time visiting with his family as well as touring the major sites of London. The highlight was our day at the British Museum and the glorious marble sculptures from the Parthenon in Athens.

The third night we traveled overnight by bus to Paris. It seems hard to remember those days before the high speed trains under the Channel. The bus left from Victoria Station, drove onto a ferry in the middle of the night to cross the English Channel, and continued the rest of the way to arrive in the early morning in downtown Paris.

I had written the Douillets to inquire about relatives in Paris and if any of them could host us. Their cousin, Mr. Bucheron, an older gentleman, offered his apartment near the Arc de Triomphe. Mr. Douillet misunderstood that I was traveling with a companion and it caused one of my first international hospitality incidents. With a few phone calls, we were allowed to stay in the guest room together. I would have slept on the laundry room floor to stay in this Napoleon-era apartment.

It was an incredible location to explore the city. Susan and I looked forward to spending our time with the treasures of the Louvre. On our visit, we focused our time on the antiquities, the Egyptian, Greek, and Roman collections. I always said that modern art began with the Renaissance.

As we were ascending one of the great staircases of the palace, a soft voice in a familiar Southern accent called out, "Look, honey, he has the same camera."

I turned to see a petite woman and her husband.

They both moved to where we were walking, introducing themselves and that they lived in Texas. They told us they were on their "trip of a lifetime" spending the entire summer touring through Europe. The couple, like so many Americans, had delayed this trip until they had both retired. The visit to Paris was almost a month into their trip. As she broke off and started talking to Susan, he asked me about my camera.

I no longer had the pocket instamatic camera from my high school trip to France. In 1982, I saved up part of the money from my summer job and bought a Canon AE-1. That 35mm camera served as my constant companion for almost twenty-five years. I could tell you the story of every scratch and dent on its body. In 2006, I relented and moved to the digital age, purchasing a Canon Rebel. I traded in my AE-1, actually getting more for the camera body than I had paid for it all those years before.

We had the same camera. He had purchased it for their trip and had never learned how to change the film. Nor did he want to learn. Whenever he came toward the end of a roll, he and his wife would begin to search for someone with a similar camera. He asked if I would change his film and I agreed.

While I changed the film in the camera, the wife cornered Susan and they began to talk. Susan kept looking over at me and smiling as they talked. Just then, I saw the woman reach out for Susan's left hand and look at her wedding ring, cooing as she did. She came running over to us and exclaimed, "Ooh, I understand that you're on your honeymoon. We waited so long to come on this trip. I'm so happy that you did this when you are still young and have your lives ahead of you!"

She lowered her voice, acknowledging that we would be in different schools when we resumed our studies in Athens and Galatas. She continued taking both our hands in hers, "I know that you'll be separated when you get to Greece but the time will pass so quickly. You will be back together soon enough."

Her voice caught in her throat as she looked at her husband and took his hand. In the meantime, I finished changing the film. And, with hugs, we parted, never to see one another again. Susan and I were changed that day. We were different people for the rest of that trip, as a couple, not just solo travelers together. Even though we were never romantically involved.

Several days later, we took the overnight train to Italy, arriving in Milan in the early morning. We visited the cathedral the morning we arrived. I still have a picture of Susan covered in pigeons when we fed them in the square before the church. Next to Venice, then Florence, Naples, and Rome. As we checked into each hotel, I could feel their eyes drift over our hands.

The day we flew to Greece, we visited the vast Vatican museums in the morning. We were pushing our time to check out of our small hotel. Realizing that we had no time to walk back, we hailed a taxi. As she paid the driver, I ran into the lobby to check out. The startled desk clerk demurely asked, "And where is your lovely wife?" I know I blushed as Susan came through the door.

We grabbed our bags and headed for the airport. Arriving in Athens, we checked into our hotel, again, under the scrutiny of the rings. The desk clerk, as we turned over our passports, asked why we did not have the same last names. We told the whole wedding story and that we had just married. Our trip was planned too quickly to have the passports changed.

We had one night together in Athens before I needed to catch my ferry for Crete to start my program. We had a recommendation for a restaurant called Thespia, near the Theatre of Dionysos, and shared our last meal, set among an arbor of grape and bougainvillea, tables of fresh Greek food, and resinated wine. The restaurant is still in operation and I have visited it every time I return to Athens.

The following day we visited the Acropolis before I went to catch the ferry in the afternoon. She accompanied me to the dock. Just like the scene from *Casablanca*, she turned in her hat and walked away toward the subway station.

We did see each other again when we were both in Athens that summer. We even had dinner with our university advisor while he was in town from his excavations – her wedding band put away and mine back on my right hand. Lives returning to our pre-trip status with never a second thought.

The planning for the summer began much like any other trip. The first twist was traveling with someone whom I knew, though had never spent much time – much less being together nonstop for almost a month. The decision to pretend to be something we were not just added a whole other dimension. We had hoped it would allow us to share a room without question, but had no idea the other questions that would be raised about us.

I felt almost embarrassed about the questioning in the first encounter. We had not rehearsed anything. No wedding or honeymoon story. All the things that everyone wants to hear. We made it up on the spot and hoped for the best.

Nevertheless, it worked. People see what they want to see. We perceive others using our frame of reference so that they conform to our norms and beliefs. It fits our perception of the world. After all, we say that perception is reality. Well, it is, at least *our* version of reality.

For me, I had a full-time relationship waiting for me at home. My roommate had been my lover since the end of my second year. He was a year younger than me. In those days, our relationship was hidden, like it did not exist. Marriage was never even a thought entertained for the two of us.

Thus, it was so ironic when I was pretending to be married. A ceremony that he and I would never partake in. Susan was fully aware of our relationship and our situation – and the absurdity of our ruse. When we were traveling, only the two of us knew that side of the story. To the rest of the world, we looked like every other young couple on our honeymoon.

They were all fooled so easily with our appearance. Everyone we met looked at us and our hands and made the leap that we were married. And nothing could be further from the truth.

How often do we look at the world in the way that we want to see it? I often believe this the way that we make order of our lives. We make neat little categories and everyone has a place, with even our own place in it.

It makes things easy, but not always right. The world is a messy place. Full of things and people that fit between the cracks of our categories. I remember the time I called the trans-woman at the pharmacy "sir" to my great embarrassment. My Southern need for respectful titles just slipped out. She responded to me, using the word "ma'am" very loudly. And not very graciously, though I did not deserve any grace.

I needed her to fit into my view of the world, someone is either one or the other. Not in between.

I like the work of categories. A place for everything and everything in its place. But that is not our world, our world is full of in-between. We do not have to look very far, just look at ourselves and we will find that many things about us are in-between. The old roles that we grew up with no longer fit. We were taught that there were certain roles for men and others for women. But, today, men are stay-at-home dads and women run corporations. Not the roles our grandparents envisioned, but the right one if we are to find our best selves.

We all know this struggle, this struggle to be our best, most authentic selves. We all have pushed the boundaries to ensure that we can become who we truly are, no matter the cost. Usually at the expense of relationships, our parents, lovers, and friends.

This struggle actually frees us. When we travel, we wake up in one place. Through the transportation of a car, a train, a plane, and the struggles to get there, we find ourselves in-between two places. Ah, but when we arrive, the joy of a new city or a familiar face makes it all worthwhile.

The sliding scale of our in-betweenness opens us to the world of possibilities, taking us places we have never imagined. Allowing us to express ourselves in ways that we never considered. We have the opportunity to transform ourselves and, in turn, our world every day. We have to seize that chance and own it.

Lessons in Traveling with Friends

—

Traveling alone means you are free to do what you want when you want. No matter our preference, we all find ourselves traveling with someone else, a partner, a relative, or a friend. It is important to consider your choice carefully and make plans to accommodate different personal and travel styles.

Before you make the first step in planning your trip, think about your travel partner's personality type. Have you ever spent a whole day or overnight with this individual? What do you know about their daily routines? Make sure to understand their eating and sleeping habits.

Most importantly, make a list of your goals for the trip and communicate them clearly. The cities you want to see and the activities you want to participate in while you are there. One may love being indoors and visiting museums all day, while another loves sports and outdoors. Be considerate and ensure that you accommodate each other's wants and plan a balance of activities.

Budget is the next thing to consider. It sets the tone for the style of transportation, accommodations, dining, and sightseeing. If you are going to be sharing expenses, work out a system of keeping track to settle up at the end.

When planning, remember not to overschedule your trip and try to do everything you both want to do. This is a sure way to make you both unhappy. Some time to be alone is important, whether resting or in activities. Make sure you have a plan on how to meet back up. And never disappear without telling the other person.

Understanding one another's packing needs will also affect how you can travel. Heavy luggage and train travel should never mix.

Choosing accommodations can often be a lengthy discussion. Consider whether you share a bedroom and bathroom. A kitchen if you plan on cooking. Focus your search on the area most convenient to the places you want to visit.

Once you begin your journey, keep in mind to listen and be respectful of each other's feelings. Travel is enjoyable but unplanned circumstances can also make it stressful. Flexibility is the key to happy travel with others.

You would be surprised how often that rings true for relationships outside of travel too.

THE REST IS HISTORY

W ith the scholarship money in hand, and the gift of an airline ticket from my parents, I was financially set for the summer in Greece. A place that I had studied and dreamed since reading Greek myths in grammar school. I just needed acceptance into the program.

On March 8, 1983, Niki Strovrolakes, director of the summer study and classics professor, sent her congratulations on my admission to the summer session in Greece. A two-page mimeographed letter (the precursor to photocopies) on printed letterhead paper. The left side contained a list of the board of directors, all well-renowned professors in their fields.

The letter opened with detailed directions from the Athens airport to the village hotel several hours away. From the Athens airport to the port of Piraeus, where to look for the two-hour ferry to the Aegean island of Poros, and the dock where the fishing boats left to cross to the village of Galatas on the mainland.

She recommended packing lightly, "with drip-dry, easy-care clothing and a warm sweater and slacks. Good, sturdy shoes will be needed for the sites, sandals otherwise. Two bathing suits and a beach towel will be handy."

Who would not dream of a study program where you need two bathing suits?

A short discussion of electricity voltage, currency, travelers checks, and college credits followed.

It closed with a request to "sign the enclosed release form and return it with your initial payment of $400 by the end of March to confirm your reservations and participation. The remaining $800 will be due by May 21st."

The second page detailed the schedule for the summer, classes during the week and field trips every other weekend. The alternating free weekends were our own time for study and travel. Over the course of the summer, we saw most of the archaeological sites, both major and minor. School began with a week traveling in Crete. There was a weekend at the ancient palaces of Mycenae and Tiryns and attending a Greek play at the Epidauros Drama Festival. A long weekend in Athens to climb the Acropolis and tour the National Museum. A week through the Peleponnesian peninsula to visit Corinth, Sparta and Olympia. The sacred site of Delphi ended our time together.

She enclosed several postcards of Galatas. Typical Greek scenes of whitewashed village streets, brightly painted fishing boats, lush lemon groves in full fruit, and the clear Aegean sea. One of the hotel exterior, white washed, blue shutters, three stories, with a plaza in the foreground.

That was it. Until I arrived in June, these two pages formed all I knew about what to expect of my summer. There was no Internet at the time to learn more about the village or the school. Every night, I went to bed dreaming of my upcoming time in Greece. I had to travel simply on faith and instincts, trusting in the just-enough information in the letter.

The year before, the James Bond film *For Your Eyes Only* was released. Using Greece as a backdrop, the film featured an archaeologist excavating the ruins of a submerged temple in the blue Aegean sea. For my eyes, Greece was the star of the film, the actors playing in front of it. These images filled my head as I arrived at the airport in Athens.

For all my imaginings, Greece delivered. A dry country of high mountains plunging their way into the sea. The ruins of dazzling white marble temples stand amid olive and citrus groves – how they must have looked when they were new. White painted villages. Markets of fresh vegetables, eggplant, tomatoes, cucumbers, locally made yogurt and honey, lamb, and goat. Fresh seafood from the fishermen on the shore, their daily catch still in their boats on ice, octopus drying on the fences in the sun. The little Greek Orthodox church in the middle of the village, its ancient icons saturated with the smell of candle wax and incense.

If you meet a Greek person anywhere in the world, just ask them about the village in their home country. They will describe the village and its streets, where their family resides. I decided to choose Galatas as my village if anyone would ever ask me. And I had the pleasure of living there for an entire summer.

We were housed in a small hotel overlooking the town square on one side and the sea on the other. Students shared double rooms on the village side. Hotel guests in the rooms with the water view. Seven brothers and sisters ran the hotel. They cooked and served food, they checked in guests and cleaned their rooms, they provided maintenance and booking services. Along with us, they and their families also lived in the hotel. A loud and busy place full of life.

I did find my way into the kitchen with the sister chef, Eutaxia, helping with meal prep and to learn from her cooking. This time her name and her recipes are recorded in my travel journal. Every summer, I make her Greek salad, Greek pasta dish, and kabobs.

The village was full of life also. The butcher was directly behind the hotel, his family lived over the shop. My room faced their apartments. I was never late for dinner. The butcher's wife, every night at the same time, called her son Basil to dinner. I can still hear her voice – I never had to check my watch.

There were thirty students in the program. Some came to study and learn, others to have a good time. All American college students, several of them with Greek ancestry. Their parents wanted them to understand the world where they grew up. I was attracted to these students, the ones who bridged my American experience with the modern Greek world. They were a living link to those myths and stories I had read.

Because they spoke Greek, they were able to navigate village life more easily. They also gave me a chance to practice learning modern Greek. We often traveled as a pack, seen together at lunch or the beach. We even attended church together, bringing us closer to the life of the village. During that summer, we were invited to a wedding and a funeral. Since none of us had the clothes to wear, the villagers came to our rescue.

Like all college students, we spent a lot of time in the street cafes and bars discussing the current state of the world and how we planned to become part of it. As rising seniors, we had one year left of adolescence and study. We spent that summer dreaming of our life ahead.

. . .

Our academic building, located a short walk outside of town, sat on Stavrolakes family land of lemon and olive trees. Its plan shaped like a pinwheel. The roofed center housed a library, the arms of the pinwheel walls created open-air classrooms surrounding the center. The library contained scholarly archaeological works in many languages, largely consisting of excavation journals of Greek sites. A substantial collection of Greek fiction and poetry rounded out the collection.

The classrooms had two walls and a stone floor, open to the sky. Simple circle of chairs and a folding chalkboard in the corner. It rarely rains in Greece in the summer. A sudden thunderstorm serves as the rare exception. In this space, I would take classes in ancient city planning, art history, and modern Greek.

Having studied drawings and maps, my city planning class came to life when we visited the remains of ancient towns. Each contained an open marketplace, a great theater, a high acropolis with its temples, as well as quarters for working and living. I was quickly able to identify the common elements by sight.

One of the first cities we visited was the ancient city of Troezen, a short hike from Galatas. Most of the site is covered in lemon groves, making it a peaceful spot where very few visitors come. Little is left of this once prosperous city. Only the stones lying on the ground serve as reminders of the important buildings that once stood there among the trees.

The foundation stones of a healing center lie on the edge of the ancient town, near a spring. Healing centers, not common in the Greek world, were actually temples; this one dedicated to Asklepios, the Greek demigod of medicine. It is believed that he was such a powerful healer that he challenged the gods' authority over life and death. Not always a smart thing to do.

His most famous temple, located at Epidauros, a site some forty-five kilometers away, became the important healing center in the ancient world. People traveled the length of the known world to be cured. The temple at Troezen provided care and cures to the local population, like a modern regional hospital does today.

The temple consisted of two halves, an open-air pool and a dormitory for sleeping and cures. The layout of the temple represents the two steps of treatment for a patient.

The first was a purification stage. The patient bathes and eats a special diet for a few days. Once purified, the patient moves to the dormitory to sleep for the night. In dreams, the god would visit the patient, giving knowledge of their disease and the instructions for curing upon awakening. Describing the dream to the temple priests, a treatment would be devised. Mostly it involved certain diets or exercises. An early form of a spa treatment. The reason for the high success rate of cures.

The temple site is open, with no fences in the middle of the groves. I went back to my Greek American friends and told them about the temple. Could we go out there and spend the night? See if we have any visions? We met with our professors and the director of the program. They encouraged us to try the ancient cure.

We decided on the next weekend. Most Friday evenings, we went to a place down by the bridge to dance. A group of players would gather. Locals would bring wine to share and the dancing would begin. The bridge was on the way to Troezen. That Friday evening, we brought beach mats and towels, extra wine and morning pastries stuffed in backpacks to make our way after dancing.

As the evening of dancing began to wind down, we headed up the coast road. We made our way in the darkness, the sky full of stars and a bright moon. I remember passing one house, able to see through the window into the darkened bedroom. A gold icon of the Madonna and child lit only by a candle encased in red glass hanging on the wall. We left the road and made our way through the groves to the ancient dormitory.

We sat up late, watching the moon set, finishing the wine and talking. We talked about Asklepios and his visitations, and about those who had come to this very place in expectation. About their faith in dreaming and cures. We talked about our own expectations for the night and our hopes in dreaming. About what weighed on our minds. We were acutely aware it was our last summer that was truly ours to enjoy. In the wee hours of the morning, we slept and hoped that Asklepios would make his visit.

The next morning, a tractor going down the dirt road woke us from our sleep. Not a comfortable sleep, but we all dreamed. We shared our breakfast and our dreams. I do not recollect any of them, not even mine. They brought all of us a sense of peace, of hope, and of clearer purpose.

For me, I had plenty on my mental plate. The summer before my last year of college had many open-ended questions. *Would I take a job or attend graduate school? Where would I live after college? What about my current relationship?* The basis for all these inquiries revolved around who I would turn out to be when and what my purpose was in this world. I am afraid to admit that I am still unsure of the answer to those questions. I am still a work in progress.

When I was younger, I thought that one day I would have all the answers. If I lived long enough, I would have more answers than questions. Life would get easier. As I aged, I realized that it does not work that way. Life seems to get harder for some reason. I spent six months journaling about this very question, trying to understand why life gets more challenging even when we think we know more answers?

The answer, it turns out, is simple. The questions simply become harder and more complex.

I rationalized it using Maslow's hierarchy. Abraham Maslow published a paper describing the hierarchy of human needs, usually represented as a pyramid. At the base of the pyramid are the most basic of human needs. I remember in my twenties when all I cared about was having enough drinking money on Friday after rent and utilities had been paid. Looking back the questions, the answers were pretty basic, though they did not seem so at the time.

Over the years, I moved up Maslow's scale in higher emotional and personal needs. The desire for belonging with friends and lovers, the need for self-esteem in my accomplishments of school, work, and community. Ultimately making it to self-actualization. At this stage, we ponder the deep questions around our ultimate purpose and fulfillment in our lives.

We all look for meaning in our lives, the ability to make sense of all the random things that happen around and within us. We are all called to an intentional life. These questions become very complex, possibly needing the gods to help us figure it all out.

I firmly believe in the power of dreaming, with or without divine intervention. Dreams are associated with the power of rest for healing. The power of letting something simmer overnight in our brains before we act on it. We are all guilty of making snap decisions, some we live with and some we regret.

Rest and dreaming allow us to make better choices in the long run. Dreaming is a key part of my relationship with my husband. Since we met, we set aside every Saturday as a dreaming day. For the whole day, we dream about anything with no fear of critique. He is good about not critiquing, though I am getting better.

We are trying to figure out how to create more space in our house in the north Georgia mountains. The small 1950s cabin has two bedrooms and two baths, more than enough sleeping space. We want more living space.

We have envisioned adding a large screened-in porch to the house. With the moderate climate of Georgia, it will provide a place for entertainment and dining, complete with a big stone fireplace for the cooler months. Over the course of countless dreaming Saturdays, we have designed and redesigned it, liking it more and more at each turn.

The porch is no longer my dream or his dream, but a collective dream for the two of us. Hammered out with patience and care. In our dreams, we already live in this soon-to-be-built space.

Rarely are we afforded months to make a decision. Usually we have five minutes. Or less. Some determinations can be made in that length of time.

Our world calls us to move on and get to the next commitment.

For other deliberations, it takes as long as it needs to get it right. Right for us or for those affected by the decision. There is a reason we are often told to "sleep on it." Everything often seems clearer in the morning light.

The school in Greece no longer exists as it was the dream of one person, Niki's dream. She grew up in the village among those lemon groves and delighted in introducing so many young people to her home. I learned later that she died at the young age of forty-six, three years after I attended her school. Like so many things we build, her dream did not outlive her and the program ceased shortly after.

Life is hard. And shorter than we can imagine. Dreaming keeps us childlike. Like making a wish on a birthday cake. I challenge you to set aside time in your life to dream, time to sleep on the big decisions in your life.

Your next dream might just cure what ails you.

Lessons in Overcoming Jet Lag

—

Jet lag is a common threat to productivity when traveling, whether for business or pleasure. We want to maximize the precious time we have and enjoy every minute of our trip.

It is very important to start your trip well rested. There are always last-minute tasks to complete before you board the plane. Start your planning early. Chip away at your action items a few every day and complete the day before you travel. Get a good night's sleep on your last night at home.

Once you board your flight, set your watch to the new time. You want to get mentally on the new time as quickly as possible. Most devices, such as phones and laptops, will update automatically when you arrive.

On your flight and upon arrival, stay hydrated and eat light meals. On the flight, they will serve food every couple of hours, whether you are hungry or not. Eat only what you want. No clean plate club here. I often save the sealed packets of cheese, snacks, nuts and sweets if not eaten. I drink plenty of water, limiting my alcohol intake.

I recommend resting and relaxing on your flight. To sleep, I use noise canceling headphones or earplugs and eye masks. For short flights under eight hours, I try my best to sleep without any sleep aids. For long flights over ten to twelve hours, I will take a sleep aid that requires a prescription. While I never sleep the entire trip, it will keep me from becoming so fidgety. Your physician can offer you the best guidance here, as I am no doctor.

When I arrive, my goal is to immediately function on the new time zone. Get right to sightseeing or work. Eat light meals and snack at the proper times. Resist the urge to take a nap. I find that sunlight helps me adjust, spending as much time as I can outdoors as possible. Caffeine can give you a boost in the morning and afternoon slumps.

At the hotel, I make the room as comfortable for sleeping as I can, setting the thermostat to a comfortable temperature and adjusting the bedding to a comfortable level. Silencing phones and other objects that may make noise. The body naturally makes melatonin to induce sleep. I take the supplement to trigger sleepiness just before bedtime, often reading in bed till I fall asleep. Melatonin is available over the counter at your pharmacy. I take it for the first couple of days of the trip as well as on my return home.

I find that I have plenty of energy on the day of arrival and the day after. The third day is the day I do not want to get out of bed. I fight the urge and plan something special that day. I find that the next day, I wake refreshed and well adjusted to the new time.

PEARLS OF WISDOM

In 1991, I took my first international business trip. While I had taken domestic trips for work, I had never traveled many time zones with jet lag to function. It was a skill I would put into use many times over my career.

After earning my graduate business degree in 1990, I took a marketing position with Hitachi Telecommunications in a suburb of Atlanta. I started interning with them between my first and second year of school. They then offered me a full-time position upon graduation.

The state of Georgia and Japan have a long history of joint commerce, dating back to the 1960s. Many Japanese companies began to locate manufacturing plants in Georgia, and by the end of the 1970s, fifty-five companies had offices in the state. This growth prompted a group of Georgians from business and academia to form the Japan-American Society of Georgia, an organization still thriving today.

The organization's main purpose is to bridge the cultural divide and create mutual understanding of the histories and traditions of both. Its big event "JapanFest" was created in 1981, beginning as a biannual event called "JapanWeek." In 2023, the event hosted over 17,000 attendees, the largest event of its kind in the Southeast.

The majority of the Japanese companies have locations along the northeast corridor of Interstate 85 outside Atlanta, with a stretch of industrial buildings and manufacturing facilities. These companies also brought their own executives who lived near their offices in large suburban homes. This was a far cry from the traditional Japanese housing their companies provided in Japan.

Hitachi was part of the Japanese corporate immigration, with over 1,000 subsidiaries worldwide. Think of General Electric and its many branches of manufacturing in years past. To name a few, Hitachi manufactures energy, construction, and automotive equipment and parts.

I worked for the North American headquarters of the telecommunications division. While we focused on phone systems, one of my first assignments was the launch of a new machine that could fax, print, and scan at the same time. Traditionally we sold products to corporations; this machine was targeted to the early home office. Walmart became our first distributor.

I worked closely with the hardware and software engineering teams on the concept and design of the product. Many of them were graduates from Georgia Tech. All of the interns, except me, were engineering students attending a work-study masters program at Tech. I was the lone business student from Emory University. I quickly learned that I needed to understand the basics of the technologies if I was going to keep up around the office. I thought, *Hey, I read Greek! This has to be easier than that.*

I had patient teachers along the way. Maybe more like translators since I lacked the basic vocabulary to understand tech speak. Over time, I gained a foothold and, before long, I could geek out with the best of them. A new language to add to my resume. The head of the software engineering group, Charlene, and my boss, Lynda, both spent a great deal of time with me. They met at Tech and were best friends since. It was no accident that they worked together, offices side by side.

Charlene traveled to attend the annual conference of a subcommittee of the International Organization of Standardization (IOS), which created standards for the Open Systems Interconnection (OSI) model. The OSI model provides a framework so that all technology systems can share data among themselves. In a sad bit of irony, after all the work to create the standards, the framework was never adopted and has little value today.

In one of our technology sessions, she confided in me that she was pregnant and asked if I would consider attending the conference for her. She had attended the last meeting in Rome; the upcoming meeting would be held in Hong Kong. She felt confident that I could represent the American division well along with our counterparts from Japan. It did not take a second for me to agree to go, though I had a big learning curve before I left.

And my education began. I left the business realm and plunged into the deep end of the engineering pool to prepare for the trip. With less than a month before I traveled, I had no idea what to expect. I had never been to Asia, never traveled internationally for business, and definitely was not an engineer. Charlene assured me I would be fine and the team from Japan would support me.

Japanese companies are true loyalists. They support each other, buying each other's products to ensure success in a region. The same is true for my airline ticket on Japan Airlines. A business class ticket from Atlanta to Hong Kong in August. Summer in Hong Kong is monsoon season and I packed as best I could for changing weather. In those days, you wore a suit every day to work. A selection of suits in various grays along with coordinating ties in bright colors and white shirts. I took jackets for dinners.

The first leg of the flight from Atlanta left mid-morning. I would arrive at my ultimate destination before midnight the following day, almost twenty hours in the air. A very long time to be seated, even in business class. The flight took me from Atlanta to Seattle, next to Tokyo and then south to Hong Kong. I was thankful for the breaks to stretch my legs, and I even got a quick shower and a change of clothes in the lounge in Tokyo.

The flight to Seattle was a Delta codeshare with Japan Airlines (JAL). In Seattle, I picked up a JAL Boeing 747. The attendant took my jacket and helped me store my carry-on. As I settled into my window seat, she asked if I would like an American or Japanese lunch after takeoff. I chose the Japanese menu for the flight. *When in Rome,* as they say.

I felt I had become fairly proficient at the local cuisine, since there was always Japanese food in the office. Raised in a culture of absolute hospitality, all visiting engineers would bring a box of sweets or snacks, sweet mochi or Kit Kats, salty nori snacks, or wasabi peas. All business lunches and dinners were multi-course affairs at local Japanese restaurants. I remember eating jellyfish for the first time after many cups of sake. Corporate celebrations in the breakroom consisted of Asahi beers and overflowing trays of sushi. I was an old hand at this cuisine.

A petite Japanese woman, immaculately dressed in a pale blue Chanel suit and pearls, took the aisle seat next to me. We exchanged greetings, using most of the Japanese that I had learned at work. The flight departed on time and service began. After drinks and snacks came the first course, a large bowl of udon noodles. The attendant placed it in front of each of us.

The Japanese engineers always told us that noodles were slurped, the louder the better. I took this as a joke, one that would get me at some function to make a spectacle of myself. As I looked at the bowl and the woman next to me, I thought that this would be my chance to see how a native does it.

Sure enough, she placed her chopsticks into the warm liquid broth, fishing out the thick udon noodles. As she held them aloft, hovering over the bowl, she leaned over putting her mouth onto the noodles. To my surprise, this motion was followed with a loud sucking sound, clearly heard over the sound of the jet engines. I was amazed that there was still air left in the cabin.

I decided to follow her lead, making happy slurps at the delicious soup. We bonded over the food and talked through much of lunch. She was returning home from a month-long visit to her sister in Canada. When we landed at Narita, I watched her family envelope her. She waved me farewell as she headed down the terminal. I still had six more hours of flight to Hong Kong.

. . .

Leaving Tokyo in the early evening, we landed near midnight at the old Kai Tak airport downtown. Most of the flight was in the dark over the Pacific. The tiny territory lit up the night, the tall buildings crowding the shores of Hong Kong harbor. We circled the city for a landing on the narrow strip of runway out into the bay. An experience, as the plane landed, it flew between the buildings. They formed a trough, with shorter buildings below and taller to the side, so that planes could land. I could see laundry hanging on the balconies of the apartments we passed as the plane descended toward the airport.

Hong Kong before the handover to the Chinese was a feast for the senses. Tall skyscrapers tower over British colonial buildings on Victoria Island. The green ferries plowing to all points around the harbor. The Peninsula Hotel with its fleet of Rolls Royces guarded the tip of Kowloon with its view of the harbor. The noon-day gun salute, reminding everyone in the territory of its allegiance to the British Empire.

I had the first day to explore and acclimate to the time change before the conference started the following day. I met the Japanese team at the hotel for dinner and we made our way across the harbor to the Cantonese seafood restaurant at the top of Victoria Peak. Nothing prepared me for the view, the electric-lit city below, the lights of the boats and ferries of the dark harbor and the constant flow of landing planes.

During this time, I learned the four major cuisines of China. Hong Kong is known for Cantonese, meats and fresh vegetables quickly tossed in a very hot wok. Most Americans are familiar with Cantonese cuisine, served in most of our Chinese restaurants. The other cuisine we know well is Szechuan cooking, lots of spices and peppers in dishes like Kung Pao. The other two cuisines, less well known, center around the cities of Beijing and Shanghai. I set out to try all four of them on my visit.

The conference started with large plenary sessions and working breakouts. Just as Charlene said, the team helped me through the days. I took lots of handwritten notes to share on my return. This trip was well before the days of email and I had no communication with the office.

Not, however, before mobile phones. Phones rang everywhere. Walking on the street and sitting on the ferries. Those old brick-shaped phones. On my last day, I took high tea at the Peninsula Hotel. I remember the large tea room with its formal setting. I could have been anywhere in the British world. The room was filled with young, well-dressed women in groups of four having tea. Beside each one was a phone, constantly ringing, filling the entire room. They would answer, chatter and then pass the phone around the table before hanging up. Every table repeated this over and over. It was the first time I had ever witnessed this very common sight today.

The conference ended on Friday. The Japanese team took flights home that evening. I decided to fly home on Sunday. Given the international date line, I could get home on the same day I left. Plenty of time to get to work on Monday. I always tried to maximize the time on my trips. Many people like to leave at the last moment and head home the instant their work is complete. They have the opportunity to see these interesting places and rarely see more than a meeting room. They travel to arrive home on Saturday with a day to recover before work. I would rather suffer through jet lag on company time instead of my personal time. Extending my work trips through the weekend would become a standard for my whole career.

The working sessions allowed me to meet the other attendees from all over the globe. I met a gentleman named Kedem, who worked for an Israeli telecommunications company. He was not leaving until Saturday and we decided to have dinner Friday evening. He had been recommended a seafood restaurant within walking distance of the hotel. With the help of the concierge and a good map, we made our way there. The dining room was lined with huge tanks teeming with fish. As an order was placed, the kitchen staff would pull the fish from the tanks. They would shortly be on a diner's plate. Nothing fresher than that.

After a long meal of dinner and drinks, we went back out into the streets. A long walk back to the hotel would help settle our large meals before sleeping. As we walked the streets, the vendors would call out to coax us into their shops. They called out to tourists – the first time I was so obviously not a local.

As we passed one of Hong Kong's many jewelry shops, we were motioned inside. In a sing-song way, the proprietor touted his jewelry as the best in Hong Kong. At nearly midnight, we both initially declined. Kedem came to Hong Kong to buy pearls for his wife and had already purchased them. Nonetheless, Kedem could not resist the thrill of bargaining, and so we were drawn into the store.

For those looking for pearls, this was the place to buy them. Hong Kong remains the world's largest importer of pearls, fashioning them into jewelry for export. The jewel craftsmen are world famous. I thought it would be a good way to learn about the trade from observing.

We were motioned to sit down, as jasmine tea appeared on trays. After pleasantries about our hotel and dinner, our business in Hong Kong, the proprietor launched the first question, "What are you looking for?"

Kedem replied, "I don't know. Just looking. Nothing in particular." Kedem knew exactly what pearls he wanted before he arrived in Hong Kong, but that strand was purchased and locked in the hotel safe.

"Who would wear my jewelry?" Do you wear watches?" he continued.

"Well, we can see what you have." Kedem said.

He began to pull out items from the cases. An

assortment of rings, watches, and necklaces – all more beautiful than the last. Glowing in the perfect lights of the store.

After a half hour or so, he started to get agitated. "You don't know what you want. You don't really want anything. You are just wasting my time. Just get out of my store."

On cue, we were escorted onto the street. We heard the door slam, the deadbolts click, and the window shade pulled down. We were uninvited. We looked at each other and started down the block. *Nothing lost*, we thought.

By the time we reached the end of the block, we heard a set of hurried footsteps behind us. "Sirs, sirs," a voice called. We turned to find the tea server requesting we return. "My boss requests that you return to the store."

Mostly out of curiosity, we turned and returned to the store. We were met with a hearty welcome and round of beers. The proprietor leaned over the counter and looked directly at us. "Now gentlemen, I know that you are looking for something. You would not have come into my shop. What is it that you want?"

Kedem calmly replied, "A twenty-three-inch strand of eight-millimeter Mikimoto grade AAA white pearls."

"There," he said, "now I know what you want to see."

Once more, he began to pull out jewelry. Strands and strands of pearls, all different shapes and sizes. Graduated sets. Colors from almost black to gray to pink to white. Kedem looked all of them over, feeling them, looking at them in the light.

"Let me show you my best pearls," he said as he started toward the back of the store. In the back room, he pulled out a beautiful set of white pearls with one large black pearl in the center. "Here is my most prized strand of pearls."

He brought them to Kedem, who rolled them over in his hands. Looking at them in the light. "These pearls are perfect. They are the most beautiful pearls I have ever seen," he started. Then he hesitated and continued, "Almost too perfect. These pearls are fake."

The proprietor jumped from his chair, pushing it over and started to scream at both of us. "What do you know about pearls? I have been selling them for years! How dare you come into my store and offend me, telling me that my pearls are fake? Do you see the Hong Kong tourist sticker in the window? I would never get that certificate if I cheated customers. Get out of my store."

He grabbed us by the collars and shoved us out the door onto the street. This prompted the now familiar routine of the door slamming, the deadbolts clicking and the window shade pulled down. Once again, we were uninvited. Kedem looked at me. "Those pearls were too perfect. I know they were fake." I could not help him there and we started down the block.

As we approached the end of the block, we heard a set of footsteps shuffling behind us. "Sirs, sirs," a voice called. We turned to find the tea and beer server requesting we return. "My boss requests that you return to the store."

"We are not going back. It is late and we have nothing more to discuss with him." Kedem said.

"Please, please come with me," said the server.

Purely out of curiosity's sake, we again turned and headed back to the store. As we entered, the proprietor started with the same rage about how he was so offended and had never been treated this way. If there was a way to turn in a customer to the authorities he would do it. He still held the strand of pearls in his hands.

Kedem held up his hands and said "I don't need this. It is after midnight and I have an early plane to catch."

The proprietor approached us, raising the pearls over his head, he said "Do you know what I think of these pearls?" With all his might, he threw the strand across the room, hitting the wall by the door. The filament snapped and pearls went scattering across the floor.

"They are fake. Now let's get down to business," he shouted.

This time the server locked the deadbolts and lowered the shades. This time we were locked in, not out. The proprietor smiled and laughed. "Come into the back vault and let me show you my finest jewelry." We followed him into his vault, a table and chairs in the center of the room. He opened drawer after drawer of jewelry.

"Here are the pearls you are looking for," he said, and handed the strand to Kedem. With a mutual trust established, he offered an incredible price for the strand. I knew what Kedem was thinking. He had no idea what he was going to do with a second set of pearls. I could not resist. Of course, I had to help out a friend.

"I will buy them," I said. "I will take them for my mother." Throughout the course of the night, I also bought a beautiful amethyst ring for my sister. Kedem also picked up several pieces for his family members. The proprietor decided that we needed a full education and explained each piece and how to look at its quality.

Nearly three o'clock in the morning, we started our way to the hotel. Hours after we left the restaurant. Kedem and I said goodnight, each to our own rooms. The next morning he was gone. I am not sure that he even got to sleep before his flight.

I woke up the next morning and checked the hotel safe to make sure that I had not dreamed of the events of the night before. The pearls and ring were still in the safe.

Upon reflection, it was the first time I had been thrown out of a shop. Much less twice in the same evening. Besides the obvious theatrics, what amazed me most was the negotiating skills that came into play between Kedem and the proprietor. First, the shop owner knew his jewelry and had a reputation to uphold within the business community. Kedem, on the other hand, needed to be almost as well-informed about the pearls he was looking to purchase. This mutual knowledge creates an understanding to arrive at an agreement.

We often hear the Latin phrase "Caveat emptor" or "Buyer beware" when we buy things that we negotiate at a yard sale, a car dealership, or online. The buyer and the seller work from similar knowledge points on product, quality and price in order to reach a mutual agreement.

Even before the first encounter, Kedem had done his homework. He knew his pearls – the size, color, grade, and length. Most importantly he knew the value and the price he was willing to pay for them. When challenged and offered the fake set, this knowledge helped him determine if they were genuine.

How does genuineness enter into the human part of the story? We say that people are genuine when they tell the truth. And trust forms the basis of all relationships.

When entering the shop for the first time, we were unknown entities, both the proprietor and us. Truly a chance meeting in the street. We sized each other up in that brief encounter. While the relationship began as transactional, we searched to find common ground among our hidden intentions.

On our second interaction, we went deeper. The place where we began to challenge each other, finding out if our intentions were true and whether to invest more of ourselves. Often, there is a test of character, whether of our own making or from others. The test sometimes leads to mistrust, but it can also be a simple misunderstanding.

When we returned for the third time to shop, the misconception was resolved and genuine trust was established. We reconciled, with trust firmly established, and the relationship was now possible to move to the next level.

For anyone who has ever watched a Hallmark

movie, one can recognize their familiar, formulaic plot.

When we travel, we invest a lot of trust in people we have just met. We have recommendations from guidebooks and online sources, but no first-hand knowledge. If I dine in a great local restaurant in a city where I will spend several days, I will go back and try different foods on each visit. Often at the recommendation of the wait staff or the owner in a small place.

Closer to home, we perform this relationship dance daily. A new co-worker on the team. A new parent in the carpool rotation. We will need to develop a level of trust as they will help us get through our days. While these people may turn out to be our new best friends over time, there are others that we have established and cultivated for years. We have labored over these relationships, deeply rooted in trust. In their presence we are allowed to be our most authentic selves, without any fear or judgment.

Take a moment and celebrate all the relationships in your life, ones that began yesterday or years ago. Savor those around us that we have taken the time and energy to trust closely. Those relation-ships that allow us to be completely comfortable in ourselves. You might even re-evaluate ones that you have discarded perhaps a little too quickly.

There is a simple test to tell if pearls are genuine. Rub the pearls across your teeth. If they feel smooth and glide across the surface of your teeth, then the pearls are likely fake. The fake perfection of some-thing only a machine can make. Real pearls have a rougher texture, even feeling sandy or gritty. The surface uneven from the natural mother of pearl the oyster has gradually placed over the impurity.

Deep relationships are a lot like genuine pearls, immensely valuable based on their rarity. A little flawed at the edges. Solid and lustrous on the in-side, built-up layer upon layer over time. And at the very center, the random grain of sand that started the whole process.

Lessons in Successful Bargaining

—

The evening in the Hong Kong jewelry store was my first experience with bargaining outside of the

US. In many parts of the world, bargaining is the way consumers buy everyday goods and services. I remember a village in the Thai jungle where I bargained (briefly) for a pair of handmade teak serving spoons. The bidding started at $2 a piece, but in no time, I had worked her down to 50 cents for both.

If you would rather not bargain, many locations have fair trade shops with set prices for locally made items. Shopping this way, you are assured the artisans receive a fair exchange for their work. I enjoy them for more reasonably priced items. If you want to learn to bargain, I would start on inexpensive things, like my spoons.

First, I make sure that bargaining is acceptable where you are shopping. It is very common in street markets and some shops, even for higher priced objects. The places you can bargain will surprise you. I have done it in the Paris flea market.

You should also familiarize yourself with the currency and be able to work the general exchange rate in your head. Many places prefer US dollars or Euros. Cash is king for getting the best price.

Once an object catches my eye, I try to study the

market, finding similar items and asking the seller their price. Almost all sellers will start at the same number. This "list" price gives you the basis to start a negotiation.

When ready to purchase, I will find a shop that carries the items of interest. Upon entering, I engage the shop owner with polite conversation. It is a great idea to learn basic polite greetings in the language. This gesture puts the owner at ease and will likely praise you for making the effort to speak the language. Engage in a conversation while you are pretending to browse.

When you locate the item, seem interested but look indecisive. Let the owner make the first offer, likely the "list" price. I will typically look slightly surprised or disappointed at the price, quickly saying I was thinking more about 25 percent of the price. The negotiation has begun.

Work until you get a price that you are willing to pay. Be willing to decline the purchase if you do not agree to the price you want. Even when walking away, you may be surprised at what happens next.

DRIVEN TO UNDERSTANDING

In the mid-1990s, my partner at the time was a commercial interior designer. Though based in Atlanta, his company was one of the premier hotel designers in the world. Their designs always evoked the feel and history of a city. He bid on a design for a new hotel in the old European quarter of Istanbul and won the assignment. He would be overseeing the project from groundbreaking to completion, spending many months between Atlanta and Istanbul. With my love of ancient cultures, I felt like I had won also.

Istanbul began its life as Byzantium, a village founded by the Greeks in the seventh century BCE.

A thousand years later in 330 CE, the Roman emperor Constantine created a new capital city, one to replace Rome. Constantine brought treasures from all over the empire to adorn the city. His belief in Christianity dotted the city with grand churches, many which still stand today. This new city Constantinople remained for a thousand years as the capital of the Roman empire. Today, we call it the Byzantine Empire, named after the original village. Unlike us, they always thought of themselves as Romans. In 1453, Sultan Mehmet breached the city walls and made it the capital of the Ottoman empire for the next 500 years. The twentieth century ushered in the Turkish Republic.

So, I ventured into this melting pot of European and Asian cultures, both ancient and modern. Delta had started a seasonal direct flight between Atlanta and Istanbul. And I had a free place to stay with my partner. I could come and go as my vacation allowed over a two-year construction period.

Istanbul, with its international airport, was the starting and ending point of every trip. I spent my first visit wandering the city, *Blue Guide* in hand, trying to resurrect the city of Constantine. Most of the Roman buildings have disappeared or been incorporated into other buildings. The ones that survived were those given a second life under the Ottomans. Churches became mosques, many with their dazzling mosaics preserved under layers of plaster. The great underground cisterns continued to provide water. In the original Roman city squares are their monuments, standing obelisks and stumps of towering columns.

In my search for the ancient tradition, I fell for the capital city of the great Ottoman empire. The progression of large mosques, each trying to outdo the architecture of the large sixth century CE church of Aya Sofya. The sprawling palace of Topkapi with its pavilions and water fountains. The grand bazaar built shortly after their arrival. Streets lined with antique wooden houses.

It was in one of those neighborhoods along the Bosphorus I found myself in search of another sixth century CE church/mosque. The overhang of the houses opened up and there it stood in a small square. I found the doors locked and no visible sign of its daily use as a mosque. Several boys were playing soccer in the street. I approached them with one of the few Turkish words I knew, "açık" or "open," and made the international sign for turning a key, then pointed at the mosque. Off they ran and minutes later, they returned, dragging an older man jangling a set of iron keys with him. For a small gratuity, he opened the door and I had the place to myself. The church, called in Turkish küçük or "little" Aya Sofya, served as a model for its larger famous cousin up the hill.

My time in Istanbul only piqued my interest to see more of the country. The ancients called Türkiye Asia Minor and it was the heart of the eastern Greek city states. The site of Troy, during the great Trojan War, stands not far from Istanbul itself. I backpacked through this region, making my way from Istanbul to Ankara by bus, train, and the occasional back of a truck.

For the next trip, I chose the southwest coast, the ancient Greek kingdoms of Lycia, Caria, and Ionia. Hayat, the secretary for the builder on the hotel project, was willing to make calls to help with in-country planning. Remember there was no Internet at this time and rudimentary email.

I planned a route of ten days that would cover some of the greatest cities of the ancient Greek world along the coast, including one of the seven wonders of the ancient world, the Mausoleum of Halicarnassus. Also the home city and church of St. Nicholas. Roughly a trek from modern Antalya in the south of Türkiye to Izmir in the west.

Using *Lonely Planet* and Michelin maps, I plotted out the itinerary and route, allowing for one or two major sites a day. Once mapped out, Hayat made all the calls for the hotels, booked the domestic flights and secured a car and driver. I would be greeted at the airport by a gentleman named Erdinç. Living in Izmir, he had driven for the NATO officials for years and, since retirement, for travelers like me.

I flew Turkish Airlines from Istanbul to Antalya, a short flight of little more than an hour. The windows were open in the small airport, allowing the salty warm air from the Mediterranean into the terminal. As I passed security, I saw Erdinç holding a handwritten sign with my name. Dressed in a suit and tie, similar in size to me but a generation older. He greeted me politely and took my bag. It was the last time I handled my bag for the rest of the trip.

On the way to the car, I realized that I had used all the English he knew. He was fluent in Turkish, proficient in German, and spoke very little English. I, on the other hand, spoke fluent English, and a smattering of German and Turkish. I thought this could be an interesting ten days. We put my bag in the trunk. I proceeded to the front passenger door. He immediately stepped to the rear and opened the back door, motioning for me to sit there. I followed his lead and made myself comfortable, feeling a little like *Driving Miss Daisy*.

He took me to the hotel in Antalya for the night. He had my itinerary and driving route to follow for when we started out the following morning.

As the extrovert that I am, I had to try to communicate with him. Using my limited German and Turkish, it proved useless and we resorted more to hand signals than words to communicate.

He did take it on himself to start to teach me the

Turkish names of things we encountered along the road. First, I learned the names for driving directions, turning left, right, and slowing down. I learned the name of every flower, vegetable, and farm animal we passed. Donkeys, cows, sheep, ducks, and chickens. Tomatoes and cucumbers. Olive and fruit trees.

I knew the names of many Turkish foods and he set about to expand my knowledge. I remember stopping at a roadside restaurant, one where you went into the kitchen to choose your food from the pots on the stove. He made me tell the owners all the different dishes along with their main ingredients, praising me like his own child.

I did learn that he grew up in Izmir, had a wife, and a son who was studying English at university. While we attempted to have higher conversations, it usually ended in futility with neither understanding the other. I wanted to know more about this person in the front seat, more about his life and family, his career, as well as the famous people he had chauffeured.

We did share one thing, the love for his beautiful country. Most sites in Türkiye are in total ruin.

With my city planning background from my summer study in Greece, I took photocopies of the excavation plans, complete with all the major buildings. Little was left of most except the foundations. Even with little to see, the Greeks were masters at siting a city, with incredible views of the sea or the surrounding countryside. When we arrived at a site, I would indicate the time I would likely return. He would stay with the car.

Near the city of Fethiye late on the afternoon of our third day together, we crested a hill to be met with a sign for one of the sites. I told him to turn left. He stared at the steep dirt road and refused, obviously worried for the safety of his car. I remained firm in my demand and he eventually relented. As we descended, a small village on the turquoise blue coast came into view. Pulling into the village, the children surrounded the car and followed us to the main square of town. Fishing boats, now empty of their catch, lined the shore at one end. Several men sat near them.

As I exited the back seat, Erdinç looked around, seeing nothing except water, shrugged his shoulders. I smiled and walked toward the boatmen. I said "Batık Şehir," Turkish for "Sunken City." They smiled, pointed to their boats, and we set off bargaining for a price of a tour. Once reaching an agreement, I motioned for Erdinç to come with me. He shook his head firmly and pointed at the car and the ground. Not budging. I pointed to the boat and motioned for him to get in. At last, he relented. I moved into the boat towards the front; he sat toward the motor with the boatman. They immediately struck up a conversation.

As we pulled away from the pier, the boatman pointed over the sides of the boat into the water. Erdinç and I leaned over and immediately saw that the seafloor was covered with regular shaped stone blocks. These blocks were the remains of the "Sunken City," the once thriving Greek port city of Dolichiste. During the second century CE, a series of earthquakes lowered the land level and submerged the entire city.

In the clear Aegean waters, we could see the foundations of buildings, staircases, and cut water channels. Piles and piles of broken clay amphorae dotted the sea; these had been huge pots used to transport wine all over the Mediterranean. I pondered those who had lived there and their fate after the quakes. An abandoned place where time slowly stopped, left frozen for us to see.

Upon return to shore, Erdinç smiled and exclaimed "Çok güzel!" The Turkish exclamation at seeing something astounding. This phrase I knew well from our time together. We returned to the car and started our trek back to the main road. We tried in every language we knew and every hand gesture we could make to express our common wonder.

For the remainder of the trip, Erdinç was the first out of the car when we arrived at a site. We performed our ritual of setting my time to return and I took off. He would chat with the guard and then begin to wander into the site. I would always return to his excitement, complete with hand gestures and Turkish words that he attempted to teach.

With two days left of the trip, we arrived in his hometown of Izmir. He pulled into the drive of the hotel and parked, carrying my bag to the front desk. I was scheduled the following day to see the ancient city of Sardis, an hour east of Izmir. The forecast called for rain and, to be honest, I had seen my fill of remote ruins for one trip. Through the bilingual desk clerk, we communicated my desire to sleep in and visit the few ruins within walking distance of the hotel. He could have the day off and pick me up the following day to take me to the airport.

. . .

The next day was rainy and I was content in my choice. On the way to breakfast, the desk clerk flagged me down and told me that Erdinç had called. He wanted to know if I would join him at his family home for a late lunch. His wife and son, who spoke English, would be there. I was delighted. The desk clerk phoned Erdinç and confirmed the time.

Erdinç arrived mid-afternoon and drove me to his apartment block not far from the hotel. He took me up to his apartment. While modest in size, it has a beautiful view of the sea. Removing my shoes, I entered his home and was greeted warmly by his wife and son. I had learned enough greetings to be considered polite. And we moved to the dining room, a low table with no chairs, sitting cross-legged on the floor.

His wife brought in dish after dish, including appetizers, cooked vegetables, and stewed meats. I was most surprised to see large green lima beans, one of my favorites. I am not sure I have ever seen them outside the southern US. In Turkish fashion, the men were seated at the table while she ate in the kitchen.

The conversation began immediately. The son, with his excellent English, served as interpreter, hardly getting to eat any of his lunch. Erdinç launched into questioning. "When Dirk says this word or phrase in English what is he saying?" I asked the same question about phrases in Turkish. It was like lightbulbs of understanding were flashing all over the room. Before long, we wished to know more about each other, the person with whom we had already spent days sharing so much.

Erdinç had never traveled that far from his hometown. All the things we had seen were new to both of us. He wanted to ask questions about all of them. I wanted to know everything about a Turkish household and customs. The three of us talked over anise-flavored liqueur well into the evening. His son performed the tireless job of interpreting for the two of us. At nearly midnight, he drove me back to the hotel.

The next morning Erdinç arrived at the hotel to take me to the airport. After my awkward Turkish greetings, he took my bag and put it into the trunk. We rode mostly in silence, the language we had perfected throughout the trip. When we arrived at the airport, he insisted to take my bags and me all the way to the check-in counter. There to say our goodbyes. I stood for a moment, in silence once more. With all the Turkish he had taught me, I realized that I had never learned the word to say goodbye. We sufficed with the international embrace of a hug.

He watched me until I passed security. I waved at him before I turned out of sight, he waved back, and I was on my way.

Today, writing around love languages appears to

be prolific. When I go online, there are articles and quizzes about understanding and identifying your specific love language, whether as the giver or the receiver. What surprises me is that Gary Chapman published the concept in 1992, over three decades ago. Something about it must resonate with people and endure.

He created the concept of love languages in his series of books on *The Five Love Languages*. In his series, Chapman set out to define the languages regarding human relationships. He identified five ways in which people express and receive love from another. While these were first written to explain the relationship between couples, he has broadened to include relationships with children and extended family. Even relating them to singles and co-workers.

The concept identifies five simple love languages:
- Words of affirmation
- Quality time
- Receiving gifts
- Acts of service
- Physical touch

Looking over the list, only the first, words of

affirmation, uses human speech to convey its "love." The rest are acts of "love" and largely unspoken.

I think about the way in which Erdinç and I interacted, the basis of our relationship. While we were truly at a loss for words, we managed to understand one another and take care of one another's needs. To show our "love" as Chapman might look at it.

Erdinç had an amazing knack for anticipating my needs. He showed his "love" through acts of service. I never waited on him in the morning or at a site. I never opened a car door or carried a bag. He sensed the things that I needed and was able to provide them before or as I needed them.

I could sense his intense love for his native land, his pride in its history and its culture. I refused to let him miss out on an opportunity for him to experience the wonders that I had traveled so far to see.

Are we ever amazed at having lunch with a good friend with whom we have lost touch? Perhaps we haven't seen them in a year or many years. We greet one another, not with words, but a bear hug and the widest smile, maybe even tears. Then come all the words. Like dropping the needle on a long forgotten record, the words just flow. Like we had our last conversation yesterday.

We say so much with our actions. Just like our words, we have to choose them wisely. Our heart knows the right things to say. Let it speak loudly. And show others how much we care for them.

Reconnect with someone in your life, someone you have lost touch with and think about often. Now is the time to do it. Use whatever gift of language you possess and show them how much you "love" them.

In those early days of emails with only phone numbers and letters for reaching out, I never thought to get his contact information. I did not enlist his services directly. As I got on the plane, I knew that I would likely never see him again. I never have.

But if I do, Erdinç will greet me with the warmest welcome and invite me to dine one more time.

Lessons in Languages

—

While traveling in Türkiye on another trip, I came into a village on the back of a truck carrying vegetables. For the next leg of my journey, I was trying to figure out the time for the bus on the following day. I could not find anyone who spoke English, so I asked if anyone spoke French. Minutes later they brought an elderly man to me who spoke enough French that I could get the information I needed.

The time you spend learning any language will always help you. And when you travel, it can be very important to know some of the basics.

Think of the way that you started learning the language in high school. You parroted phrases, repeating them over and over with your teacher and other students. Similarly, I use the same method to learn common travel phrases.

The most common phrases I try to learn and practice. I have learned these in everything from Israeli to Thai. Try to learn phrases to express the following:
- greetings (hello, good day)
- small talk (how are you, my name is ...)
- politeness (thank you, I'm sorry)
- Common situations (phrases dealing with transportation, restaurants, and hotels)

I also find that learning numbers will help, especially when it comes to money, dates and times. I focus on one through ten, but being able to count to 100 is always helpful.

Most guidebooks contain a language section containing these phrases, typically near the back under useful travel information. If it does not have one, you can search for travel phrases in the language on the Internet. Often, these will have audio clips to assist you with pronunciation. There are also apps that will allow you to communicate in both written and spoken forms.

I would only purchase a phrase book if I am there for an extended period of time.

INTO THE WILD

T he town of Killarney, Ireland is the last place that I hitchhiked. Or, for that matter, even had the courage to try it.

It began as a typical business trip in the late fall, leaving Atlanta on Friday evening and landing at Shannon Airport on Saturday morning. I made my way through the small airport and picked up my car for the drive south on small Irish roads to Killarney, no more than a two hour drive from the airport.

Killarney serves as the essential stop for every tourist to Ireland as well as every tour bus. In summer, the streets become clogged with walkers, cars, and buses navigating its narrow streets. Set in a beautiful valley surrounded by lush mountains, Killarney sits on the shore of a series of lakes cascading from the mountains. I spent the rest of the day exploring, staying overnight in a lovely bed and breakfast in the residential area outside of town. I am hardly the first American to visit Killarney.

Another American, William Bourn, came to Killarney in the early 1900s and assembled a 25,000-acre estate of mountains, woodlands, and lakes as a wedding present for his daughter, Maud. Upon her death in 1929, her parents and her husband gifted the property to the new Irish State in 1932. The Bourn estate formed the bulk of Killarney National Park, the first national park in Ireland. Her portrait hangs along with her husband's in Muckross House where they lived.

The park makes one of the best places to hike in Ireland if the weather cooperates. And on Sunday, I was in luck. The morning dawned warm and sunny.

From reading my guidebooks, I had chosen to hike the Gap of Dunloe in the National Park, about ten kilometers outside the town. Since my body was still on East Coast time, I woke very early and had breakfast. I drove around the end of the lower lake. On the way, I made a quick stop to visit the ruins of the medieval church of St. Finian with its fine view of the lake and Killarney town.

From there, I continued to the start of the pass, parking in a large lot with several other cars. Kate Kearney's Cottage stands there, providing food and drink to walkers today as it did when it became a park. The Cottage forms the gateway for the path up to the head of the gap, a rise of nearly 600 feet. The paved path is largely closed to car traffic, making a perfect place for walking. I started the climb with other walkers. Jaunting cars, two-wheeled carriages pulled by horses, take those visitors who are unable to make the hike. The clopping and neighing signal their arrival along the path.

The road curves through farms and fields full of sheep and wildflowers. A swiftly running stream tumbles through six lakes, deep black pools set in the green landscape. The steep mountain sides, full of gorse and rocks, narrow as I climb. Most of the walk stays at one level. Ascending a set of switchbacks, I climb to a second level. Once there, I could see the head of the gap not much farther above me. I reached the gap before lunchtime.

I stood at the gap and looked down both sides, wondering which way to go. I could retrace my path back down the way I came, which was the familiar path back to the car. Or I could continue on, down a winding switchback path that led down through Irish farmhouses, white with their slate roofs, to the far end of Killarney's lake. Consulting my trusty guidebook, I read that there was a boat that left every afternoon from Lord Brandon's cottage on the lake and went back to town. I could always find a way to get back to the car from town.

Since it was still early in the day, I made the choice to continue down the other side of the gap, slowly making my way through the switchbacks until I reached the woodlands of Killarney Park. Following my book, I traipsed to the cottage and the pier where the boat would arrive. It was now about one in the afternoon.

While I waited, I ate the lunch I had packed for the walk. I pulled out my bread and cheese, making myself comfortable on the dock. Several other hikers walked past while I waited. One stopped and decided to talk, an older gentleman with his dog out for an afternoon stroll on a warm fall day.

"What are you doing there?" he called out.

"I'm waiting on the boat back to Killarney," I knowingly responded.

A big grin came across his face and he said to me "If you're waiting on the boat, you better make yourself comfortable. This boat won't arrive for months till spring."

He then offered options to get back, the best course of action that I could return the way I came.

Since it was approaching midafternoon, I was at a loss what to do. If I walked back the way I had come, it would take almost five hours to return to Kate Kearney's Cottage and my car. I had only the map in my guidebook to make my next move. It is hard to imagine those days when there was limited, if any, mobile service in the rural parts of the country. Today, in the world of smartphones and almost universal coverage, I could click an app that would pinpoint my exact location and order a car service to take me anywhere I wanted to go.

Without these conveniences to help me, I decided to continue forward to the main Killarney road, even though there was no direct road or path. I started through the woods in the direction of the road where I could also hear the random cars passing. Eventually climbing out of the woods. I reached the side of the road and began to walk toward town. Within a half hour, I passed a road sign that marked *Killarney, 17 kilometers.*

There was no way I was going to reach town before sunset. Again, I was faced with another choice. I summoned the courage to do what anyone would do in the same situation in a country not their own. I stuck out my thumb and hoped that it was an international sign for transportation help. Cars whizzed past me on the narrow road. I was constantly straddling the ditch to get out of the way of the cars. As one travel writer says of Irish roads, "There is not your side of the road, nor my side of the road, there's just the road."

Just when I thought it was hopeless, I heard the loud rumble of a tour bus behind me and I jumped to the bank to make sure that it did not hit me. To my surprise, the bus slowed in front of me and came to a stop. I ran up to the front door, catching my breath. The door swung open and the smiling driver looked down at me.

In a warm, Irish accent, he asked "Where you headed?"

"Killarney." I said "I'm trying to get back to town."

His face darkened slightly and he spoke more seriously. "Well, the girls and I have decided that we'll give you a lift under one condition. We want you to sing a song or tell us a joke. Once we hear it, we'll decide if we'll let you ride."

I had recently heard a great joke – even one that you could tell in mixed company. It was a clean, Irish joke in which the locals come out on top. I took my best shot and began to speak, telling the quip in its entirety. There was a moment of silence. I waited, holding my breach. Then the entire bus roared with laughter and applause. (I know you want to hear the joke, but I am going to make you wait until the end of this chapter.)

"Get on the bus," he said. "We do have to make

one stop at Torc waterfall, but we'll get you to Killarney."

As I settled onto the bus, I realized what he meant as "girls." They actually were girls. These young women were from a high school in Cork city and were spending their winter break traveling the country. They were travelers in their own country. I sat in the middle of them and we talked about places I had visited, where I was walking today, where they were going and a little about their school and favorite subjects.

We arrived at Torc waterfall and hiked the short distance, an amazing drop of water into a deep ancient forest. Upon returning to the bus, we quickly made the short drive into the middle of town. The driver parked the bus and told the students to enjoy the town and return to the bus in a few hours. He asked if I would join him for a pint at a pub he knew, almost across the street from the parking lot. There I learned about his life, growing up in Dublin, getting his bus license, and shuttling tourists, both foreign and Irish, around a country that he had learned so well by driving it.

I finished my beer and I said goodbye, but my journey still had one more leg. I had to get back to my car, still parked at the gap. I walked to the taxi stand, asking the first driver if he would drive me there.

Shaking his head, he declined politely. "No, it's too far at the end of the day."

"What if I pay you double, for your trip there and your trip back?" I followed up. Again, he declined.

I thought I would try with the second taxi driver. I asked the same question I had asked the first. To my joy, he agreed that he would take me if I paid the double fare. I was on the final leg of my daylong odyssey. He dropped me at my car, easy to find since it was the only one in the lot. I paid the fare and waved him off, happy to be back where I started. I set my bag in the back seat, ready to head to Clonakilty to start work on Monday morning, although not before I stopped a taste of Kate Kearney's cottage pie and a cold Guinness.

In an odd way, I knew relatively where I was. I was never lost. I even knew how to retrace my steps and get back to where I started. With the map, I generally had an idea of how to trek on to Killarney.

I could hear the noise from the road, but I was simply at a loss on how to get there in the amount of time that I had.

I made the choice to move forward, rather than retracing my steps. As I stepped off the bus, I was struck with the boundary between the manicured path and the wild woods, the known and the unknown.

To our ancestors, the wilderness meant many things, most of them frightening. A place of danger and fear. A place of separation and isolation. A place beyond civilization.

When they settled in a new place, they would clear the land. They laid out roads, then built homes and plowed fields – places of order and safety. They whispered about the creatures who inhabited the woods and feared them. Even today, we tell ghost stories in the light of a campfire.

The wilderness was a place where they buried their dead, outside the boundaries of civilization. In contrast, when they built their great places of faith, they chose the wilderness. Think of the temples of Egypt in the desert. The oracle of Delphi on a high inaccessible mountain. Stonehenge on the wide empty Salisbury plain.

The wilderness was not just a place for the scary and the lifeless; it was the dwelling place of the gods. Those who came before us found courage to leave the comfort of familiar settings and venture out to find their own inner paths.

This ambiguity of wilderness reminds me of my choice on the shoreline in Ireland. The road's paved blacktop behind and the dense pathless woods ahead. We have to remember Irish woods are full of fairy folk and leprechauns.

I chose off-roading that day and I will choose it every time. I always know how to come back to where I started. My father would tell me as a child to return to the last place I saw him if I ever got lost. In turn, that would be the place that he could come to look for me. It always made me feel safe.

There is something about leaving the path. To muster the courage to take that chance. To see what is on the other side of the hill and to walk down it. Even once exhilaration turns to feeling a little lost and seemingly alone. Until you are found again, among friends. Friends you never knew you ever had, and whom you meet only once.

Closer to home, we have that opportunity daily to make these choices. We constantly stand between the path and the forest, though the line is not always so clear. We attempt to live our lives in an organized and structured way, because that will keep us safe. Most of these choices have minimal consequences, like choosing crunchy peanut butter rather than creamy. Others appear monumental, especially around relationships and careers. These have the potential to change the entire trajectory of our lives. Whatever the decision, I challenge you to find your courage and take the unknown path.

No matter what route you choose or where it takes you, you are never alone. You just need the courage to ask and listen for help. These words may be from your best friend, or an unknown stranger. They are more than willing to lend an ear, accompanying you on the way in and out of your own wilderness.

Over the years, I have hiked the same path over the gap many times, though I have never ventured down the backside of the hill again. I always turn around, retracing my steps on the path that I know will bring me back to the parking lot and my car. But before I turn around, I spend a moment at the top of the gap, admiring the view. My eyes often follow the path down the other side. And I remember the day I made my own way.

If you should ever make your way in Killarney and the Gap of Dunloe, make your way to Kate Kennedy's Cottage. You will be greeted as a friend at the door, no matter the route you took to get there.

A Joke Worthy of a Bus Ride

—

Here is the joke that I told to earn my admittance on the bus ride:

At an international beer conference, three CEOs find themselves in line at a bar. The first, the CEO of Budweiser, steps up and states to the bartender, "I'll have a Budweiser, the King of Beers."

Once the bartender fulfills the request, the second, the CEO of Heineken, steps up and states to the bartender, "I'll have a Heineken, the best beer of Europe."

The bartender gives him the beer as the third, the CEO of Guinness, steps forward.

He asks the bartender for a lemonade. The first two look at each other surprised. They both ask in chorus, "Why didn't you order a Guinness?"

To which the third responds, "Well, if the two of you aren't drinking, neither am I."

THERE AND BACK AGAIN

My company had begun work with Tata and Reliance Industries in India during the Great Recession. At the same time, many US companies sought to downsize and move many corporate functions to an Indian workforce. These forces pushed us to establish first sales, then operations in the country.

While there was no Indian office, the customers were supported from our European operations in Ireland. There, colleagues traveled back and forth to provide engineering, network support, and customer care. We joked that we were the only company in the world where, if an Indian customer called customer care, they would reach someone in Ireland.

Coming out of the recession as our international business exploded, several of my coworkers established homes and moved their families to India. Several Irish associates moved to provide operations support in Mumbai. A good Indian friend and colleague moved from Chicago to Bangalore to open our first office and head up our dispersed sales team.

I had always wanted to visit India. Working in technology, I had many Indian associates, both in the US and in India. In Atlanta, we would go to Indian restaurants for lunch and they would talk about growing up in Delhi and Mumbai. My financial advisor, a South Indian, became a close personal friend. On several occasions, I enticed her mother into giving me Indian cooking lessons so that I could make my own. When I decided to get married, the wife of a coworker from Kolkata offered to choreograph a Bollywood song as our first dance, a tradition at Indian weddings. Food, music, and dance are the essence of a culture, bringing it to life.

Even with repeated offers from coworkers to come and stay with them, there was never a compelling business reason to travel to India. I was going to have to make the time and pay full freight for the trip. In 2013, my partner at the time, who is now my husband, decided to take two weeks and make the journey.

I set about creating an itinerary that would cover the area of north India, from the great palaces and mosques of Mughal Rajasthan in the west to the Hindu Pradesh palaces and temples in the east.

When I asked my husband what he wanted to include, he exclaimed "elephants!" Now that I had his wishlist, I made sure to include multiple opportunities to see them along the route. For other native animals, I planned an extended stay in the forest near the Ranthambore National Park in hopes of seeing the wild tigers. Also, a day at the Bharatpur bird sanctuary.

After several days of travel in India, we arrived in the beautiful city of Jaipur. The city, known for its lavish pink palaces, serves as the capital of the region of Rajasthan. One of its unique attractions is an outdoor astronomical observatory, built in the early 1700s. While the entire garden looks like a set of giant child's play blocks, its instruments were cutting edge for the time. Its sundial stands almost ninety feet tall and accurate to within two seconds.

After a day of sightseeing, the driver dropped us off at our hotel. We bid him goodnight and told him when to meet us the next morning. Our hotel, the Narain Niwas Palace, was built in 1928 as a country residence for one of Jaipur's royal families. The same family still manages the property as a hotel today. After checking in, we settled into our guest room with antique furniture and hand-painted walls. The room's large windows overlooked the trees in the ten-acre garden of trees, courtyards, and pavilions.

I have a passion for fine hotels, previously working before graduate school as a concierge at the Ritz Carlton in Atlanta. More specifically, I love lobby bars. They serve as the perfect place to watch their well-heeled guests pass by. Several friends recommended a visit to the Rambagh Palace, once the home of the Maharajah of Jaipur.

We decided if there was any place to have a gin and tonic with ice, Rambagh's Polo Bar would be the place. Only filtered water is safe to drink in India and luxury hotels make their ice with filtered water.

We put on pressed slacks and blazers, hoping to dress the part and blend in with the rest of the guests. We headed to the gates of our hotel and into the bustling street beyond. We flagged down a tuk tuk and negotiated a price for the trip to the Rambagh.

If you are not familiar with tuk tuks, they are three-wheeled motorized vehicles that are hired like taxis. They resemble a motorcycle in the front with a covered place for seating in the back. It can carry two or three passengers. I have ridden in them in many warm-climate countries from southeast Asia to north Africa. They are a necessity to everyday transportation in India, darting their way through traffic faster than a taxi.

We settled in the back and we were on our way through the evening rush hour traffic. As we approached, the street followed the high stone walls of the hotel garden. Further down, a gap in the wall formed a gate complete with wrought iron fence and armed security. The driver pulled into the entrance way to pay the fare and exit the vehicle. As we did, a security guard approached and questioned where we were going. We replied that we were going for drinks in the Polo Bar.

He allowed us to pass and walk down the long road through the garden to the palace. We approached the large porte cochere filled with luxury cars. We continued up the stairs, asking the doorman the location of the bar.

We made our way through the hotel and into the Polo Bar. In 1930, the Jaipur polo team was at the top of their game and made a clean sweep of all the major international tournaments. The Polo Bar, a large room with painted walls and a tented fabric ceiling, was designed to commemorate their winnings. The walls were lined with trophies, old black and white team photos and polo equipment. A cozy bar at one end and tables filled the rest of the room. Busy with hotel guests.

We were motioned to a table and the waiter soon arrived. We felt it only fitting to order Sapphire gin and tonics with ice, accompanied by limes. The limes are local and in season in the winter. Over conversation, one drink became two and we were hungry. Not wanting the light food from the bar, we asked the waiter where we could dine in the hotel restaurant. He scurried off.

The bar manager returned and asked if we were guests in the hotel. When we answered that we were not, he informed us that we could eat in the courtyard restaurant. The one caveat was that we were required to spend fifty dollars. We both grinned and thanked him, aware that we had just spent over a hundred dollars on drinks. We paid the tab and headed out to the courtyard.

The restaurant turned out to be the great lawn of the palace. Gilded tables and chairs scattered before a small raised platform with two performers, one playing the stringed sitar and a traditional singer. We were shown a table and looked over the menu. We decided to share an Indian thali, a traditional meal served on a large platter that includes a variety of dishes. Typically there are vegetables and lentils, chutneys and pickles, rice, yogurt dips and bread, and sweets. Plenty for the two of us.

And as it happens, a thali costs fifty dollars at the Rambagh Palace. Satisfying the one requirement for our entry to dinner. The food arrived and we ate. The players continued to serenade us. Before finishing our dinner, the moon, which full only a few days ago, rose over the horizon and washed out the sky full of stars. Capping a magic evening, it was time to return to our hotel.

We made our way back to the front of the hotel, asking the doorman if we could have a taxi. He scurried off. We waited for about ten minutes when the concierge came to greet us.

"May I inquire how you came to the hotel this evening? Typically our guests have their own drivers," he said.

I smiled at him and said, "We gave the driver the night off and took a tuk tuk here."

These are words I had never spoken and never will again.

Now with a false grin, he replied, "Well then, that is the way you should return to your hotel."

That was all he said to us. No additional explanation. Like we were gatecrashers at a party or we skipped out of the hotel without paying the bill. He motioned for one of the security guards at the door to come where we were standing.

"Please escort these gentlemen back to the gates," he said.

His final words still hanging in the air, the guard motioned with his machine gun to begin our journey. Through the dark, the three of us walked the long walk from the hotel, through the garden. When we were safely outside, the large gates shut. We stood looking at each other on the now quiet streets, pondering the complete mystery on what just transpired.

Whenever we travel, we are bound to come across someone who does not have our best interests at heart. On the same trip, a hotel clerk double charged us for a room. I had paid the bill and went out to meet our driver. When my husband turned in the keys at the desk, he was informed that I had not paid the bill and he paid for it in cash. We did not discover what happened until miles down the road. When we called the hotel, they claimed we only paid once. The clerk likely pocketed the money.

Street scams are also very popular these days. We were almost involved in two of them. One involving a man dressed as an initiate priest at a Brahman temple and money for the temple, the other involving dung thrown on our shoes with offers to help us clean them up for money.

These things happen when you travel. You chalk them up to experience and move on. The morning of the hotel double charging, we were traveling to see the Taj Mahal. We could have let the event ruin the day. Our frustration was short-lived and evaporated within minutes of arriving in Agra. The incident was soon forgotten as we stood before one of the greatest monuments dedicated to love and a wonder of Indian architecture.

We have to put the bad situations in perspective. Just as we navigate the ups and downs of a journey, we must navigate the ups and downs of life. Adversity, whether in travel or in our personal and professional lives, is inevitable. What defines us is not the challenges we face, but how we respond to them.

Perspective is a powerful tool in overcoming the bad things in our life. It is easy for them to overwhelm us, allowing them to overshadow all the good things in our lives. However, by consciously choosing to focus on the good, we can shift our mindset from one of frustration to one of resilience. Each new day brings new experience, offering us the chance to refocus and move forward.

I am sure that I was not focused on being positive and making the best of the situation as I stood outside the locked gates of the Rambaugh. I probably felt more indignation mixed with a little bit of bewilderment. Whatever I was feeling, a call down the street shook me from my thoughts.

"Sirs, sirs, I am here. I waited for you," the male voice called.

We looked in his direction and saw the tuk tuk driver that had brought us to the Rambagh. He waved, starting his engine, and slowly moved toward the gate.

"I have waited for you," he repeated. We exchanged smiles and got into the back of the tuk tuk, grateful to see a friendly face. He drove us the short distance back to the hotel along the now deserted and dark streets.

When we arrived back at our hotel, we stepped out of the tuk tuk. Bowing our heads, our hands pressed together, we thanked him for his generosity and patience. I have no idea how much money I gave him. I know it was many times over what we had negotiated for the original ride to the Rambagh.

The gardens of the hotel were alive with people. A paper shadow puppet show of a king and his escapades was in full swing. The wordless puppets romped through the tribulations and joys of the adventure, bringing giggles and sighs from children and adults that transcended any language.

Life resembles the characters in the puppet show. Like the puppets, we have to live fully in the present moment. Each experience, whether good or bad, is a part of the rich tapestry of our lives. By embracing each moment, by savoring each encounter, and by remaining open to the world around us, we cultivate a life of meaning and fulfillment.

When anyone asks us about our trip to India, it never includes any of the bad things that happened to us, only the good. Choose to make every day a good day.

Lessons in Traveling Safely

—

We all want our travel experiences to be positive, though that is not always the case. The economies of many places rely on travel dollars and the authorities work diligently to make sure that travelers are safe and happy. On a recent trip to Egypt, I was concerned for my safety, particularly when the State Department said to rethink travel on their website. I held on to my bravery, spent three weeks and felt safe the entire trip.

As in the case of Egypt, I always research the destination through guidebooks and websites, also travelers who have been there recently. The State Department has an excellent website, though I think it tends to be overcautious. You can also register with the embassy while you are on the site. The website will also provide information on vaccinations, some are recommendations while others are required by the location. Understand local laws, particularly if you will be driving.

In your research, identify the safe neighborhoods and seek out accommodations there. Also, check hotel and apartment reviews to find if others have commented on any safety issues. No matter where you go, be aware of your surroundings. Pay attention to your environment and the people around you, especially when you are alone or in an unfamiliar area.

Limit the valuables you take on your travels. I often travel with an inexpensive wedding ring and watch, the expensive ones safely at home. Also, limit the amount of cash you carry, taking what you need for the day and leaving the rest in the hotel safe.

Know the common scams when you travel. You will stay aware if you start to feel you are being pressured into a situation that may lead you to trouble. Keep everything close to your person when you are out.

Use the hotel safe to secure anything of value: cash, travel documents, all electronics. Make copies of your passport, travel insurance, and other documents and keep them digitally or physically.

Understand the need for appropriate insurance. I keep global medical insurance. If you travel a lot, an annual membership is very reasonable. Travel insurance can be valuable for more expensive trips, particularly with tour operators or cruises. Many credit cards carry sufficient insurance for most of my trips. Car insurance is required in certain countries. Make sure to know what is best for your location.

Last, but certainly not least, is to stay connected. Share your travel plans with trusted friends and family and keep them updated on your whereabouts.

ROOM FOR ONE MORE

I found Ireland late in life. In my early forties. It was never high on my bucket list. There was no high culture. No renowned monuments, either intact or in ruins. I had no known Irish ancestors to find, nothing to help learn who I was or where I came from.

In my mind, it was a backwater on the edge of civilized Europe. How wrong I was.

On a recent trip in 2023, I brought my mother and my sister to Ireland. My mother had been with me multiple times; for my sister, it was her first trip. We were sitting at dinner when my mother posed the question of the number of times I had traveled to Ireland. I responded that I had no idea since it was nearly two decades of work and pleasure trips. She reacted that she thought that would be my answer.

Ireland is a place I have grown to love, even though my first visit was less than twenty years ago.

In mid-2005, I began working for a small technology firm in Atlanta. I headed up their product innovation and development for a line of communications software. The main US operation centers were located in Colorado Springs and Kansas City. Within a week of joining the company, I was on my way to visit these locations. The current head of operations had recently returned from building an operations center in Clonakilty, Ireland, a tax-friendly place to support our growing European business.

I booked my first flight to Ireland to visit the operations team in early 2006. I arrived on a cold, wet Saturday morning in February, making my way by car from Shannon Airport to Clonakilty. A detour into Ireland's heartland took me through much of the middle of the country.

My destination was the monastic ruins of Clon-macnoise, founded in the sixth century CE by Saint Ciaran. I arrived not long after the site opened, an atmospheric mist surrounding the place. The site of the church sits atop a green hill, overlooking a wide bend in the River Shannon. The ancient ruins are surrounded by modern graves just outside its walls. Two great stone crosses stand before the ruined monastery church. A small roofless chapel down the road represents the best of 12th century architecture in miniature. I felt transported from the hustle of our time to a more contemplative one. A true gift of Ireland to the world.

My solitude was shattered as I arrived at the hotel in Clonakilty, a leisure center as the Irish call them. A hotel that has full entertainment for the entire family, the best of a cruise ship on land. The rainy climate forces the Irish to build indoors to entertain themselves. The hotel complex hosts restaurants, pools, game rooms, a gym, and a cinema. I arrived in the bedlam of cooped-up families after a quiet day of monasticism and scenic country roads. My jetlagged body, though, was soon asleep through it all.

The noise started early on Sunday morning with the slamming of doors and children running up and down the halls. By noon, check out time, the place was silent. All the families returned to their respective homes. I had the run of the hotel for the rest of the week until they all arrived again on Friday. Time for me to venture out into this place that would become my home away from home in years to come.

Clonakilty is a small town on the southwest coast of Ireland, an hour's drive west of Cork City. A picturesque Irish village of brightly painted buildings surrounding a bay to the sea. Famous for its beaches, its music pub, De Barra's, and its black pudding. The Irish come from all over the country to spend a week in the warmer season by the sea. In the winter, it is quiet and only inhabited by locals, except an occasional business traveler.

Off the main street, I found lunch in a local pub. Cottage pie and a pot of tea in a firelit room. Afterwards, I was meeting a co-worker named Brendan, who offered to show me the *real* Ireland. At that time, Brendan was the single guy in the Irish product group and served as the self-appointed welcome committee to all visitors. As I have learned, Brendan has intense pride in his hometown and wants to share the places he loves.

I admire Brendan's sense of place. The generations of his family that have lived there. If I had to say it, Brendan is probably the most Irish of people I know. All of his family's names, including his, are steeped in the rich history of Ireland and the Irish saints.

Brendan always has a joke and taught me my favorite Irish joke. On a recent trip to his house, his wife asked me to tell the joke because she wanted to hear it told with an American accent, and even more with a Southern one. The joke goes this way:

Question: "What did Saint Patrick say when he drove the snakes out of Ireland?

Answer: "Are you lads comfy in the back?"

She and the children were greatly amused, finding the joke even funnier through my telling. It always gives me a kick to tell this joke on Saint Patrick's Day, reminding me of Brendan, his family, and his homeland.

We met in the hotel lobby to begin his tour. We

climbed into his small car and headed off along the coast road. Brendan, an avid surfer, took me to his favorite beach, Owenahincha. A long expanse of sand and rock, winter gray waves crashing into the shore. The road passes the famous beaches of West Cork. Beaches are called strands in Ireland. Broad strand, Red Strand, Warren Strand.

As we approached Long Strand, Brendan asked if I had ever been caught for breaking and entering. Before I could answer "no," he asked if I wanted the potential opportunity to do it. I did admit to him that I had gone in places that I was not supposed to be, but I had never been caught for it at this point.

Behind Long Strand are the ruins of a large castle, Castlefreke. The castle burned in the early twentieth century and belonged to the Irish Land Commission. There are paths that traverse the grounds, running back from the beach. While these had public access, the castle was surrounded by an eight-foot metal fence with a security guard positioned at its entrance. Brendan, ever clever, knew where the fence was torn open. He also knew where to stand to watch the movements of the guard. Through the fence we went and made our way to the point with a view of the guard station. When he turned his back, we, quick as a wink, were inside of the structure. From Brendan's description, it felt as though he had once lived in this house instead of simply trespassing.

Safely escaping Castlefreke, we returned to the car and continued down the coast road, passing through nature preserves and small villages until we reached the town of Baltimore. Baltimore sits almost at the end of Ireland, as far as you can go in the southwest of the country. An old fishing village, it now boasts holiday homes and a bay filled with sailboats. At the top of one of the hills stands the Baltimore beacon, a whitewashed stone structure that acted as an early lighthouse. The sun reflecting off it could be seen during the day to alert sailors of their location.

Brendan wanted to make sure that we arrived at the beacon before sunset. Rain had fallen for most of the day, but the clouds lifted as we approached the beacon. The setting sun peeked below the clouds at the horizon and the beacon lit up in its last rays. From the top of the hill, I had a 360-degree view of the countryside. Looking one way to Baltimore stood the islands and the wild Atlantic. In the other direction were the patchwork fields of emerald green.

To complete the tour, we went down into the village and went to Bushe's Bar, a pub that sits on the edge of the marina. Unknown to me, Brendan decided to conduct his own experiment by ordering two pints of stout, a Murphy's and a Guinness. Murphy's, the local stout, is bottled in nearby Cork City. Guinness, brewed in Dublin, is its world-famous cousin. Brendan did a blind taste test on the two. I tasted one and then the other. He asked which I preferred. I chose Guinness, though I did not know it. He revealed my choice. Not sure if I had upset the balance of some international relationship, he laughed and told me we would be friends for life. Over the years, he and I have shared quite a few Guinness pints.

On the drive back to Clonakilty, the rain started once more. And it continued all week from the time I arrived until I left. Brendan had offered to have dinner midweek at one of the local seafood restaurants in town. The day came. Late in the afternoon, Brendan dropped by my desk and said he was not going to be able to go to dinner after all.

He explained that he needed to go and help his father milk the cows. Brendan's aunt Nan and uncle Tommy had several dozen cows that needed milking. Tommy had injured himself and was temporarily unable to herd the cows into the barn and do the milking. Brendan and his father would need to be there for the early evening. If we wanted to go to dinner, we could go later or choose another night.

I first told Brendan that going afterward would work for me. Then, I sheepishly asked him if I could come and help them. Brendan looked surprised and agreed. With a grin, he said to wear something that I did not mind getting dirty in. I laughed as I thought of the work clothes I packed. I headed to the hotel and changed into a pair of jeans, shirt, and casual sweater, all of which could be laundered before I went home.

In the gathering dusk, Brendan picked me up and we set out for Nan and Tommy's farm. We turned off the main road onto one lane roads, finally giving way to dirt lanes lined with stone walls covered with blackberry brambles. Rivers of rain ran down the ruts in the road. In the trunk was an extra pair of rubber boots to go over my shoes. They went up to my knees. A long rain slicker covered the rest of me. At least, I would stay dry and fairly clean through the process.

By the time we arrived, Brendan's father had already gotten the last of the cows into the barn. He was in the process of hooking up the milking machines. They explained the entire process while at the same time instructing me how to hook the milking liner to the soft underside of the cow udders. While it looked painful to me, the cow looked pleased to be milked.

He told me the milk went to the local creamery to be turned into butter and cheese. He asked if I had ever had Kerrygold products, which have now become popular in America. When I see a package, I remember that milk from these cows went into the mix.

Tommy came out to the barn while we were

working. At seventy-four, he was pleased to see an American doing manual labor. Nan was soon behind him, making sure he did not hurt himself further. Brendan introduced me to them both. They reminded me of the farm families I met growing up as a teenager in rural Virginia. Salt of the earth. Tommy's almost toothless grin and Nan's girlish laughter made me feel very welcome, as the Irish say. Any friend of Brendan's was part of the family.

Brendan asked if I would help move the cows back to the pasture. We climbed onto the tractor full of feed; the cows knew to follow. We returned, closing the large wooden gate, and headed into the house to dry off and warm up. A white two-story Irish farmhouse with a slate roof, with fireplaces on each end.

Nan invited us in for tea and biscuits, better known to us as cookies. A kettle of water boiling on the stove. She poured the steaming tea into large mismatched mugs and offered milk that recently was inside the cow. She opened a package of McVitie's biscuits and spread them on a plate. As she placed them on the table, we all began to talk.

Nan asked me many questions. She asked about my job and working with Brendan. I could tell how proud she was of him. She was very interested in my time in Ireland, about the places I had seen, and what I had thought of her country. I could not help gushing on and on about her Ireland.

Then she glowed. Her response, "The most beautiful place on earth. Here? My heavens." I secretly knew that she agreed wholeheartedly with me. As we talked, the cups of tea warmed my hands and my insides. The digestive biscuits served as a sweet accompaniment to the conversation.

Now, I am a lover of McVitie's biscuits and thought I had tried them all. There is a British store in Atlanta and I make a point to stay well stocked. But these were different, they tasted like caramel.

"Nan, these biscuits are delicious. Are these caramel?" I asked.

She handed me the wrapper as I studied it. They were caramel. She nodded to my question.

"I have never seen these in the US," I said. "I will have to get some to take back with me before I leave." I said.

"Oh, I thought you had everything in America," she retorted. There was a round of hearty laughs at the table.

We finished up our tea and biscuits and said our goodbyes, complete with hugs and offers to come back anytime. After cleaning up, Brendan and I went to dinner. In all these years, I have no recollection of where we went to dinner. My journal only recounts my time in the barn, in the rain with the cows, and at tea with Nan and Tommy.

When Brendan told me about his conflict, it would have been so easy just to say, "Oh, that's great. I will meet you for dinner after you finish milking the cows." Something inside prompted me to recognize an opportunity and the courage to say, "Let me come with you." Brendan opened me to a world that I had not seen before, welcoming me into his family and to his life.

Life constantly presents us with all sorts of circumstances. First, we have to see it as an opportunity. It can be veiled inside something more mundane like my dinner postponement. Once recognized, all we have to do is walk through it. It sounds simple, though, we have to muster everything inside ourselves to say *yes* and live outside of ourselves.

When I look at life, I see that there are two ways to live our lives. One is to live out of scarcity. As a child who grew up with working class parents, we always had enough. We had to be thrifty with any extras, which were allowed only once all the needs have been met.

To live this way, I take stock of all I have, my finite resources. Then subtract all the things that I need. The remainder is what I want. Only after careful consideration can a portion be spent beyond the need. A cousin of mine has a saying she always quotes to me, "Let want and need be friends." It is something that I can never reconcile.

The other way is to live out of abundance. Abundant living always reminds me of the Leo Lionni's book *Frederick* that I read as a child. The story follows a family of mice through the seasons from spring to winter. The mice toil during the warmer months digging a burrow, gathering, and storing food.

All except one named Frederick. Instead of working, Frederick lies on his back, noticing the daffodils bloom in the spring, the grass grow in the summer and the leaves change color and drop in the fall. He is busy seeing the abundance of beauty in the world.

Then winter comes. The world is frozen and covered with snow. As all the mice huddle and shiver in their burrow, the family looks to Frederick. They beg him to tell them all about the seasons that he saw and remembered. He starts to describe the daffodils and the grass and the colored leaves. Just by his telling, their hearts are warmed and satisfied until the arrival of the next spring.

In the world of abundance, there is enough of everything. For both necessities and extras. The most precious commodity in my life is time. The time I invest in travel reminds me even more of its preciousness.

When I travel, I set aside the time to break from all the things that need to be done. A break from my routine in the place I know as home. At the time of this writing, I returned from a week at an all-inclusive resort in Mexico. Before the trip,

I was certain I would be bored stiff within three days. Within hours, I was amazed at how lounging at the pool, soaking up the sun, and reading a book are actually doing something. I would never consider those as activities at home. They are luxuries of time.

At home, it is hard to live abundantly. To do what seems to be "wasteful" with time. There is a constant stream of things that need our attention. Responding to one last work text. Picking up the children from practice. Making dinner for yet another night. Just like the mouse family. It is hard to find that time to stop and watch the world go by. It is a luxury that very few of us can afford.

The challenge is to live in abundance on our returns from travel. To remember the value of stopping, sitting and reading, and remember that there is actually more than enough time. Attempting to break away from the stranglehold of our all-consuming to-do lists.

Helen Keller said, "Life is either a grand adventure or nothing at all." These are courageous words and take us far out of our routine comfort zone.

In later years, I saw Nan at Brendan's wedding. Tommy had passed by this time. She was holding court in a group of women as I approached her. I asked if she remembered me.

"Remember you? How could I forget the young American who had never eaten a caramel biscuit?" she said with a grin. The women around her giggled as the dinner chimes rang. She asked if I would escort her to her table. I took her arm and led the way.

On my most recent trip to Ireland, Brendan wanted to show me his new camper, one that his family trots off to the continent for a month in the summer. He needed to recharge the battery before their next trip. We drove over to Nan and Tommy's house, though it is theirs no longer, both having passed away. The house, now rented, still looks the same. The renter also leases the pastures behind it to raise his own cattle. The barn where the cows were milked stands quiet except for the fluttering of birds in the rafters. The camper now parked in the place of the cows.

After taking the camper for a drive, we headed back to the car. I stood for a moment looking at the house, remembering Nan and Tommy, the rainy evening, and the warm kitchen table. It reminded me that when you think you have everything, there's always room for one more biscuit.

Lessons in Traveling to New Destinations

–

When I am traveling to a country where I have never been, I often want to make the most of my time and see as much of the country or region as I can. After the first visit, I can decide if I want to return and if I do, where I will focus my time and energy.

I keep a running list of places that I want to visit, largely based on my interests. When I get a window of time to travel, I first consider what destinations have decent weather during my travel time. The weather will determine the activities available. Traveling solo most of the time, I have the flexibility to travel in off-season and shoulder seasons.

Seasonality also plays into the price of transportation and accommodations. Flights, both for miles and for points, will fall considerably in the off and shoulder seasons. Hotel prices will also reflect the number of visitors. Any money saved goes back into the travel budget for more trips.

I consider the amount of time I have for travel. If I have a week, I will consider locations in the Americas or Europe. Leaving on Friday evening and returning the next Sunday gives me eight full days of sightseeing. If I have two weeks or more, I think about locations in Asia and Australia, since I am investing a full day of flying time. I want to maximize the time I have there, "getting my money's worth," so to speak.

Once I have decided on timing and length of time, I will search the internet for itineraries posted by fellow travelers. I am usually looking at their travel route, including cities and the time it takes to get between them. Many travelers will post the sites visited, the hotels and the mode of transportation. I even consider package tours and study their itineraries and routes.

After researching several, I begin to shape a rough outline of the trip, including cities to visit and the length of time at each. I then consult guidebooks on the country or region to begin refining the trip. I use a spreadsheet to fill in the time, changing things as I go. I also include prices that will give me an estimate for the cost of the trip.

PARTY OF ONE

On the last day of any trip, I often call it my "oyster" day. The idea comes from the phrase "The world is your oyster." On that day I often spend it revisiting places I have loved or eating food I want to experience again before I head home. To carry these experiences as my last memories of a place. Too sad to think of it as my "last" day there, I would rather call it by another word, a day to relish and remember, a true "oyster" day.

During my most recent trip to Paris in 2024, I had one such day, the day before I left. I was planning to travel alone for the trip when I had breakfast with my financial planner who, after two decades of advice, became a close personal friend.

When she asked me why I was going, I told her that Delta had a SkyMiles sale and, more importantly, the Louis Vuitton Foundation was hosting an expansive exhibition of the works of the painter Mark Rothko. His paintings were my starting point to loving abstract art, but that, as they say, is another story.

She quickly responded that she loved Mark Rothko and would I be willing to let her tag along. We quickly started to plan a trip for early March. As luck would have it, my return flight was one day after hers, leaving me in Paris alone for my "oyster" day.

Paris as always delivers on the wonder scale. My father begrudgingly visited the city for a weekend on a trip with me. He was still smarting after sixty years from his view of the French and Paris handing over the city to the Nazis during World War II. While we were there, we visited a favorite restaurant of mine, the Auberge de la Reine Blanche on Île Saint-Louis, an island in the middle of the Seine.

Above the table where we sat, there was a New York City firefighter's hat and a picture of the American flag raised over the rubble of the World Trade Center. My father said nothing and remained silent on his thoughts of the city for the rest of the trip.

Upon returning home, my mother phoned me several days later and recounted a conversation between my sister and my father. He told her that she had to visit Paris.

"Why?" she asked.

He replied, "Because they only made one of them."

They only made one of them.

On this most recent trip, my advisor and I planned a week in the city of lights. We spent a week of wonders, eating at Alain Ducasse's new boat restaurant with a view of the Eiffel Tower, and shopping at the refurbished Samaritaine department store and the Paris flea market. Even the better part of a day spent in the Mark Rothko exhibit.

After almost a week of cold rain, my "oyster" day dawned cloudless and warm. The spring weather arrived in time for one day for me. I started the day with a croissant and coffee from the patisserie down the block from the apartment. I spent the rest of the morning at the Carnavalet Museum, a grand city house recently renovated to showcase the history of Paris, from its Neolithic beginnings to the present age. I returned for my favorite lunch at a Jewish restaurant nearby in the Marais. The afternoon was for the Cluny Museum where the ancient and medieval history of Paris comes to life. The museum had also been renovated and reopened for the 2024 Summer Olympics.

As I left the museum in the early evening, my thoughts turned to dinner. And I thought of the Auberge on Île Saint-Louis. The restaurant had been a staple for good food and memories for many years. In the gathering dusk, I walked down Boulevard Saint-Michel towards Île de la Cité, past the furious repair work on Notre Dame after the fire. Swinging around to its backside, I crossed the bridge onto Île Saint-Louis and headed down its main street. The restaurant is located on the far end of the island.

I walked past and peered into the window, wondering if the food was still as good as I remembered. To my dismay, there were very few people in the restaurant. Actually only one table. I turned and continued down the street thinking whether it might have changed. It had dropped out of all the guidebooks even though the Zagat rating still hung in the window. I gave it the excuse that it was early in the evening and everyone in Paris eats late. I turned, my stomach taking over and walked into the restaurant.

Behind the counter was the woman who had been there on my last visit. She greeted me in French and showed me to a table. Sitting right by the window I retrieved my journal, the companion from my backpack and began to write. Replaying in my mind everything I had done over the last ten days of my visit. Capturing my "oyster" day on paper.

The only other people in the restaurant were at a table to my right, an older woman, a younger woman and a college-aged woman. I assumed based on family resemblance that they were a grandmother, her daughter and granddaughter. The grandmother appeared about my age. Eavesdropping on their conversation, I learned about the true relationship between the three women. The grandmother was recanting how many times she had eaten in the restaurant. She told her granddaughter the story that this was the place where her mother and her aunt had learned to eat mussels on her first trip to Paris many years ago, even pointing out the exact table.

I could not resist. I decided that I had to interject into their conversation the times that I had eaten in this restaurant. I introduced myself and said I was from Atlanta. With their familiar drawl, I learned they were from Waco, Texas. "We're practically neighbors," she said, being both from the South.

The grandmother first came there in the mid-1980s, on the recommendation from the flight attendant that the crew always ate there on layovers. It became a personal favorite after that. She pointed out the table where she and her husband had eaten their first meal. Then she called out the table that she, her husband, and their two daughters, had eaten those mussels all those years ago. Meanwhile, this trip was the granddaughter's first visit to Europe, a week split between London and

Paris. The grandmother had to bring her grand-daughter to this restaurant that was full of her family memories.

I talked about the times that I had eaten there. The first time that I came to the restaurant in the 1990s with my then-partner at that time, his memory still lingering like a ghost though he was long gone from my life. I came back in the early 2000s with my parents. The trip where my father saw the NYFD hat. The hat no longer hangs on the wall, replaced by a framed picture of a Paris street scene. My father has now been dead nearly fifteen years and his ghost also lingers in the place. All of us sitting and laughing in the large table in the back, half banquette and half chairs.

In the late 2000s, I brought my now-husband for dinner while we were both doing work in Paris. He worked for a French organization and I worked for a software company that had an office in Paris. We were very early in our relationship and that evening was filled with stories of our former trips to Paris and all the other places we wanted to go in our lives. We recently returned in 2018 after taking a trip to see the chateaus of the Loire valley. The trip ended with a weekend in Paris. We could not let an opportunity to visit slip by. The restaurant remains a special place for us. Both of those tables stood empty tonight.

My mother and I took a two-week trip to Normandy and Brittany in a cold November. We had our last evening of the trip in Paris. When asked where she wanted dinner, she asked about the place we had been with my father on our trip together years before. That evening we reminisced about the meal with my father and that table beneath the fireman's hat. He had died a few years before. To her credit, my mother is now eighty-five years old and very much alive, still traveling internationally whenever she gets the chance. That window table was empty.

I looked around the room. At the table in the window, the large table in the back and all the different tables where I had eaten so many meals with others. The tables still seated those from my memory.

As I pondered, the tables had quickly begun to fill up with diners who will create their own stories in this place. A thought suddenly occurred to me. This meal was the first one I had ever eaten here by myself.

And even though no one was sitting across from me, I was never alone.

A FINAL LESSON
IN TRAVEL JOURNALING

I always travel with a journal. On second thought, I am never without my journal, carrying it any time I will be alone for a period of time. I have always used paper and pen as my choice, and it has become an extension of my thoughts and my personality.

As I said earlier, I started with journals for traveling, written down to document my experiences on my trips. My first travel journal is a small loose-leaf notebook with lined paper, something that would fit easily in the purse or pocket of an adult. For other trips, I have used formal travel journals and simple composition books.

My current journal is leather-bound with a re-fillable insert for pages. I prefer to have unlined paper. I feel that it allows me more freedom on the page to write or draw. I also begin every entry with the date and location.

I often begin the entry with all the things I did that day, including what I ate, what I visited, and how I traveled. I also interject stories as I make my way through the day.

When you journal, describe a place or event that inspired you, any people that you met along the way and what you discussed.

Next, write about how this day is not like other days. What made this day special? How did being in this place change you? What did you learn that you want to incorporate into your daily life and practice? What is the one thing you want to remember about this day?

You can also capture your travel experiences just as easily electronically with whatever device you choose, even your phone. Follow the same line of questioning to capture your experiences.

The most valuable aspect of journaling is not just recording but being able to return to these entries months and years later. When I reread my travel journals, I am often surprised by forgotten details, experienced emotions, or observations that seemed minor at the time but later proved profound. This practice of reflection creates a dialogue between your traveling self and your everyday self, bridging those two worlds in exactly the way this book encourages.

Whether you prefer pen and paper or digital, I hope you will start documenting your own travel wisdom. The richest souvenirs are the lessons we carry home and a journal ensures they are never left at customs.

ACKNOWLEDGEMENTS

If I enjoy a book, I always read the author's acknowledgements. Most acknowledge individuals who add to the creation of the book, much like a human bibliography. I thought long and hard about what needs to be included here, since I acknowledge most of the characters in my stories either by name or association. There are some individuals I will mention later in the section, though I want to start with some general thanks before I get to those.

Words, the building blocks of communication, allow us to express our thoughts, emotions, and ideas. From the poetic verses that touch our hearts to the powerful speeches that drive change, words inspire, comfort, and unite. While powerful, they are also completely inadequate and clumsy at expressing human emotion and memory fully. All I have to do is remember the last argument to realize that fact. Nonetheless, they are the best we have and I am grateful for the opportunity to use them in my craft.

The travel, restaurant, and hospitality industries have enriched my experiences and broadened my horizons. From the warm welcome at a hotel to the delightful meals at a restaurant, these industries and their dedicated workers create memories that last a lifetime. Their unwavering commitment to guest service and comfort is truly commendable, and I am deeply thankful for their contributions to making my journeys exceptional.

Modern financial instruments such as debit and credit cards, as well as travelers cheques, have revolutionized the way we manage our finances. They provide convenience, security, and flexibility, enabling me to travel with ease and confidence. I express my gratitude for the innovations that have made financial management effortless and travel more accessible.

Maintaining a journal is one of the most reward-ing practices of my life. I began the discipline of journaling while reading Julia Cameron's 1992 book, *The Artist's Way: A Spiritual Path to Higher Creativity.* It allows me to reflect, document my journey, and preserve memories. The discipline required to con-sistently keep a journal provides me with a sense of accomplishment and clarity. I am grateful for the habit that has been a constant companion, offer-ing insights into my thoughts and experiences, and nurturing my growth.

No author can work in a vacuum and this book is no different. I am grateful that I found Ripples Media and its staff for seeing my vision and helping me turn it into a reality. You have made it so much more than I could ever imagine. To Andrew Vogel, my editor, my coach, my protagonist and antagonist, my Judith Jones. I would never have done it without your support. To Nicole Wedekind and Dorothy Miller-Farleo who helped bring it from words to production. To Burtch Hunter for his beautiful cover and layout, though most especially for being the first person to read my book and love it. To Jeff Hilimire, founder of Ripples Media and a great humanitarian in our city of Atlanta.

A special thanks to two individuals: Autumn Phillips and Stacey Blaiss. Autumn for her incredible foreword that captures the essence of my book. Stacey for her insights in choosing the best book cover. Your marketing and design knowledge was incredibly valuable in the final version.

I am grateful to the authors and those associated with books that have encouraged me along the way: Kathy Conway, Roshani Chokshi, Clint Fluker, Lasley Gober, Elizabeth Horner, Lyn Pace, Vicky Alvear Shecter, Barbara Brown Taylor, Matt Terrell, and Leslie Wingate.

ABOUT THE AUTHOR

Dirk Brown's love affair with travel began in rural Virginia, where his family cultivated his wanderlust from an early age. His first travel journal, started during a childhood trip to Disneyland, marked the beginning of a lifelong practice of capturing his adventures through writing.

Throughout his career with several international companies, he seized every opportunity to explore new corners of the world. Today, Dirk continues to travel and journal, finding inspiration in both distant lands and his beloved home city of Atlanta, where he resides in the historic Virginia Highland neighborhood.

When not writing or traveling, he channels his passion for community and art through his work with cultural institutions, affordable housing initiatives, and local organizations. His book *The Road Lessons Traveled* represents the culmination of decades of observations about how the traveler's mindset can transform our approach to everyday life, a philosophy Dirk embodies in both his writing and his living. This is his first book.

www.ingramcontent.com/pod-product-compliance
Lightning Source LLC
Chambersburg PA
CBHW031501120626
46545CB00005B/1703